# Florence

COLLINS

*Glasgow & London*

First published 1990
Copyright © William Collins Sons & Company Limited
Published by William Collins Sons & Company Limited
Printed in Hong Kong
ISBN 0 00 435777-9

# HOW TO USE THIS BOOK

Your Collins Traveller Guide will help you find your way around your chosen destination quickly and easily. It is colour-coded for easy reference:

The blue-coded 'topic' section answers the question 'I would like to see or do something; where do I go and what do I see when I get there?' A simple, clear layout provides an alphabetical list of activities and events, offers you a selection of each, tells you how to get there, what it will cost, when it is open and what to expect. Each topic in the list has its own simplified map, showing the position of each item and the nearest landmark or transport access, for instant orientation. Whether your interest is Architecture or Food you can find all the information you need quickly and simply. Where major resorts within an area require in-depth treatment, they follow the main topics section in alphabetical order.

The red-coded section is a lively and informative gazetteer. In one alphabetical list you can find essential facts about the main places and cultural items - 'What is La Bastille?', 'Who was Michelangelo?' - as well as practical and invaluable travel information. It covers everything you need to know to help you enjoy yourself and get the most out of your time away, from Accommodation through Babysitters, Car Hire, Food, Health, Money, Newspapers, Taxis and Telephones to Zoos.

Cross-references: Type in small capitals - CHURCHES - tells you that more information on an item is available within the topic on churches. A-Z in bold - A-Z - tells you that more information is available on an item within the gazetteer. Simply look under the appropriate heading. A name in bold - Holy Cathedral - also tells you that more information on an item is available in the gazetteer under that particular heading.

Packed full of information and easy to use - you'll always know where you are with your Collins Traveller Guide!

*Photographs by **Michael Dent** & **Keith Allardyce***
*Cover picture by **Travel Photo International***

# INTRODUCTION

Few cities allow you such a high degree of intimacy on short acquaintance as Florence. But despite the speed of the seduction you will find the enchantment lasting.

Part of the reason why the city's charms are so accessible is the compactness of its historical heart, the Centro Storico, in the middle of which stands the magnificent Duomo. One can cross the old city within an hour, walking at a fast pace and traversing the River Arno on the ancient and picturesque Ponte Vecchio, the only one of Florence's five bridges to escape German bombs during WW II (the others have since been faithfully reconstructed). However, if you were to stop along the way at every church containing frescoes of unsurpassable beauty, every gallery housing innumerable majestic works of art, every museum boasting important collections and every palace of historic significance, the same walk would literally take you days if not weeks. Almost nowhere else on earth, except perhaps the Vatican Museums, will one see such a concentration of artistic riches within such a relatively small area.

The emblem of Florence, the 'city of flowers', is the lily, and it was in the 14thC that the intellectual, commercial and artistic life of the city blossomed after a turbulent history of internal division, resistance to invasion from without and struggle for commercial supremacy within Tuscany. The institution of a republican form of government (the *Signoria*) composed of representatives (*Priori*) from the great merchants' guilds (the *arti*) created the stability, wealth and civic pride necessary to engender a new age of patronage in the arts and sciences. The city abounds in buildings constructed or rebuilt under the supervision of one or other of the major guilds, as well as in works of art commissioned by them. One need only look at the statues of the guilds' patron saints in the niches on the exterior of the old communal granary and chapel of Orsanmichele to realize the lavishness of their patronage, for there we can see the work of Donatello, Ghiberti, Verrocchio and Nanni di Banco. This atmosphere of creative freedom and experimentation allowed an artist like

Giotto to break with medieval tradition and introduce the beginnings of modernism in art which paved the way for other great innovators such as da Vinci, Brunelleschi and Masaccio.

By the 15thC Florence was governed by an oligarchy of wealthy merchant families belonging to the most influential of the guilds, those of the woollen cloth trade (the historic basis of the city's wealth) and the banking institutions. The influence of the bankers' guild spread throughout Europe with the circulation of a coin minted in Florence called the *fiorino* (the florin), the reverse side of which was embossed with the city's proud badge, the fleur-de-lis. But, significantly, this emblem appears less frequently on Florence's buildings than another: the *palle* (balls) of the Medici.

This famous family belonged to both of these powerful guilds and emerged as the most successful and richest merchants and bankers in the world, as well as Florence's rulers. It was under the reigns of Cosimo the Elder, Piero I and Lorenzo the Magnificent that Florence really came into its golden age, for they were both the greatest of the city's patrons, making it the artistic, cultural and scientific capital of Italy, and amongst the greatest of collectors of all time. Some of the architects and artists they employed to build, decorate and reconstruct villas, churches, libraries and palaces, and to execute works of sculpture and painting, included Michelangelo, Donatello, Lippi, Ghirlandaio, Vasari, Michelozzo, Brunelleschi and Botticelli. In turn, members of this illustrious family have been immortalized in painting and sculpture throughout the city.

With the exception of two interruptions by opposing regimes (one led by the fanatically puritanical monk Savonarola), the reign of the Medicis continued into the 18thC, and we can be thankful that the last remaining representative of the family, who died in 1743, bequeathed all their treasures, the splendid collections of art, furniture, books and manuscripts, coins, bronzes, antique gems and ancient pottery, to the city with the stipulation that they never be removed and always be accessible to the people of the whole world for their enjoyment.

If, however, you feel a little jaded after visiting Florence's overwhelming number of art treasures, then take a trip into the beautiful Tuscan countryside. The fertility of the surrounding land, with its low, rolling

hills dotted with poplar trees and charming villas, has made it one of the most famous wine-growing areas of Italy, home of the Chianti vineyards. Here too there is a feeling of history in the ancient twisted trunks of the vines and the little fortified medieval towns, some of which were immortalized by Dante in the *Divine Comedy* and inhabited at various times by Boccaccio, Leonardo da Vinci and Machiavelli. The larger centres such as Siena, San Gimignano, Pisa, Volterra, Lucca, Empoli and Arezzo can be visited in a day, while Fiesole, Impruneta and Galluzo can be 'done' in half a day and should not be missed. Although there are some discos and clubs in and around Florence, the 'birthplace of the Renaissance' is certainly not best known for its glam-

ourous nightlife. After a day of sightseeing or shopping, or an excursion into the countryside, why not relax in typical Florentine fashion by sampling the famous *bistecca Fiorentina* accompanied by a carafe of chianti in a busy, cheerful trattoria, followed by a stroll around the streets, stopping to watch the excellent street entertainers who sometimes attract huge crowds, and finishing the evening with a *grappa* or cocktail in one of the elegant outdoor cafés on the Piazza della Repubblica.

*Carolyn Donaldson*

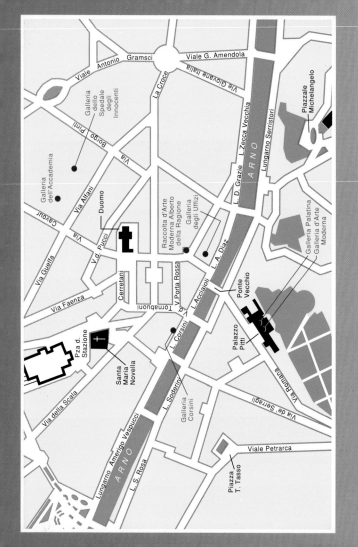

# Galleries

**GALLERIA DEGLI UFFIZI** Piazzale degli Uffizi 6.
•0900-1900 Tues.-Sat., 0900-1300 Sun. & hol. Between the Piazza della Signoria and the Arno. Entrance in left wing. •L. 5000.
*The richest collection of Italian art in the world. See* **UFFIZI, WALK 1, Uffizi**.

**GALLERIA DELL'ACCADEMIA** Via Ricasoli 60.
•0900-1400 Tues.-Sat., 0900-1300 Sun. & hol. Off San Marco. •L. 4000.
*Main exhibit is Michelangelo's famous statue of David (see* **WALK 2, A-Z**).

**GALLERIA DELLO SPEDALE DEGLI INNOCENTI**
Piazza SS Annunziata 12.
•0900-1400 Mon., Tues., Thurs.-Sat., 0800-1300 Sun. & hol. Along the Via dei Servi from the Duomo. First floor Foundling Hospital. •L. 2000.
*Adoration of the Magi by Ghirlandaio (see* **A-Z**) *figures amongst the fine Florentine paintings. See* **Spedale degli Innocenti**.

**GALLERIA CORSINI** Palazzo Corsini, Via del Parione 11.
•Admission by appointment only. On the Lungarno Corsini. •Free.
*Contains the most important private picture collection in Florence, including major works by Signorelli, Pontormo, Raphael and Rigaud.*

**RACCOLTA D'ARTE MODERNA ALBERTO DELLA RAGIONE**
Cassa di Risparmio, Piazza della Signoria 5.
•0900-1345 Mon., Wed.-Sat., 0800-1300 Sun. & hol. •L. 2000.
*Former private collection of 20thC Italian works by de Chirico, Carrà, etc.*

**GALLERIA PALATINA** Palazzo Pitti (first floor).
•0900-1400 Tues.-Sat., 0900-1300 Sun. & hol. •L. 4000 (includes admission to the Appartamenti Monumentali - see **MUSEUMS 3**).
*16th-18thC paintings, including Raphael's Woman with a Veil (1516) and Titian's Portrait of a Gentleman (c.1540). See* **PALAZZI 1, Palazzo Pitti**.

**GALLERIA D'ARTE MODERNA** Palazzo Pitti (second floor).
•0900-1400 Tues.-Sat., 0900-1300 Sun. & hol. •L. 4000.
*Contains over 2000 works of art. Emphasis on the Macchiaioli School of 19thC Italian Impressionists (Rooms 13-26). See* **PALAZZI 1, Palazzo Pitti**.

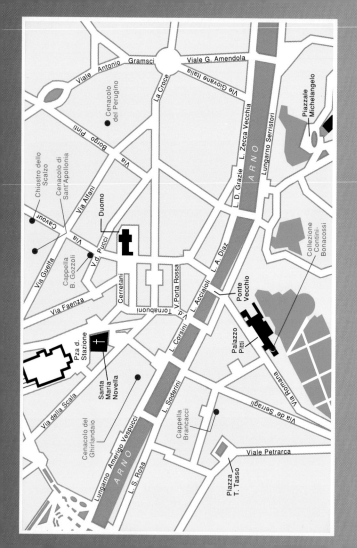

## General

**COLLEZIONE CONTINI-BONACOSSI** Palazzina d. Meridiana.
• Book visit in advance at Uffizi ticket office. Behind the Pitti. • Free.
*Collection of paintings by Italian and Spanish artists such as della Robbia, Veronese, El Greco and Tintoretto.*

**CAPPELLA BRANCACCI** S M. del Carmine, Piazza del Carmine.
• 0900-1200, 1530-1830.
*The influential frescoes by Masaccio (see* **A-Z***) include the splendid* Adam and Eve Expelled from Paradise. *See* **CHURCHES 1, S Maria del Carmine.**

**CAPPELLA B. GOZZOLI** Palazzo Medici-Riccardi, Via Cavour 1.
• 0900-1230, 1500-1700 Mon., Tues., Thurs.-Sat., 0900-1200 Sun. & hol. First staircase on right of courtyard. • Free.
*Gozzoli's* Procession of the Magi, *on three walls, depicts the Medicis and other notables travelling through an idealized Tuscan landscape (identify the artist by his initialled red beret). See* **PALAZZI 1, Palazzo Medici-Riccardi**.

**CENACOLO DI SANT'APOLLONIA** Via XXVII Aprile 1.
• 0900-1400 Tues.-Sat., 0900-1300 Sun. & hol. • Free.
*Andrea del Castagno's (see* **A-Z***) impressive* Last Supper *(1457) powerfully demonstrates his characteristic use of contrast and perspective. See* **WALK 2.**

**CENACOLO DEL GHIRLANDAIO** Ognissanti, Borgognissanti 42.
• 0900-1200 Mon., Tues., Sat. West of Piazza C. Goldoni. • Donation.
*A famous represention of* The Last Supper *by Domenico Ghirlandaio (see* **A-Z***) decorates the far wall of the 13thC refectory. See* **CHURCHES 2, Ognissanti**.

**CENACOLO DEL PERUGINO** S M. M. dei Pazzi, Borgo Pinti 58.
• Closed Sun. & hol. Ring for admission. Near Piazza M. d'Azeglio. • Free.
*Perugino's masterpiece of* The Crucifixion *(1493-96) covers an entire wall of the convent chapter-room. See* **CHURCHES 1.**

**CHIOSTRO DELLO SCALZO** Via Cavour 69.
• 0900-1400 Tues.-Sat., 0900-1300 Sun. & hol. Near San Marco. • Free.
*Splendid 16thC cloister containing a cycle of 16 frescoes illustrating* The Life of St John the Baptist *by Andrea del Sarto.*

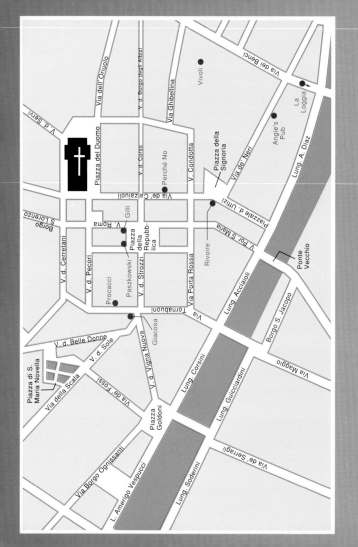

**RIVOIRE** Piazza della Signoria 5.
- 0800-0030 Tues.-Sun. (summer), 0800-2400 Tues.-Sun. (winter).
*Tearoom overlooking the Palazzo Vecchio. A favourite with British tourists.*

**PASZKOWSKI** Piazza della Repubblica 6.
- 0730-0100 Tues.-Sun.
*Sit alfresco in summer and enjoy the orchestra playing here every evening.*

**GILLI** Piazza della Repubblica.
- 0800-2400 Wed.-Mon. (summer). 0800-2100 Wed.-Mon. (winter).
*Another popular open-air café on this lively square.*

**VIVOLI** Via Isola delle Stinche 7.
- 0800-0100 (summer), 0930-0030 (winter) Tues.-Sat.,
0800-1330,1615-0100 Sun. Near Santa Croce.
*Sample the famous ice cream and don't be put off by the tacky decor!*

**PERCHÉ NO** Via dei Tavolini 19r.
- 0800-2400 Wed.-Mon. Near Orsanmichele.
*This stylish gelateria offers an astounding variety of sorbets and ice creams.*

**LA LOGGIA** Piazzale Michelangelo 1r.
- 1000-0100 Thurs.-Tues.
*A splendid 19thC setting, the best coffee in Florence and a marvellous view.*

**GIACOSA** Via Tornabuoni 83r.
- 0730-2045 Mon.-Sat.
*A café with as much elegance and charm as any in Vienna.*

**PROCACCI** Via Tornabuoni 64.
- 0800-1300, 1630-1945 Mon., Tues., Thurs.-Sat., 0800-1300 Wed.
*An atmosphere of sophisticated serenity. Truffle sandwiches are the speciality.*

**ANGIE'S PUB** Via de' Neri 35r.
- 1200-2400 Tues.-Sun. East of Piazza della Signoria.
*This popular brasserie attracts young people of many nationalities.*

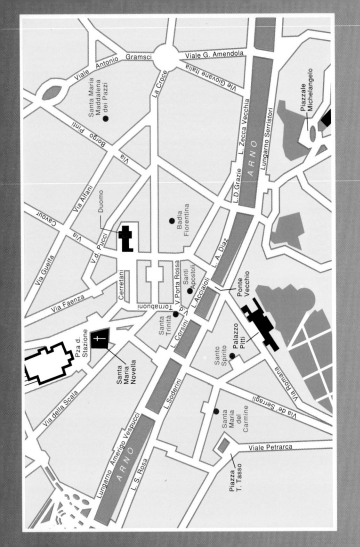

**DUOMO** Piazza del Duomo.
•1000-1700. Centre of the old city. •Free.
*Florence's magnificent Santa Maria del Fiore is one of the largest cathedrals in the world. See* WALK 1, **A-Z**.

**SANTO SPIRITO** Piazza Santo Spirito.
•0800-1200, 1530-1830. South of Ponte S Trinità off the Via Maggio.
*Behind the unassuming white facade lies one of the most harmonious church interiors in Florence. See* **A-Z**.

**SANTA TRINITÀ** Piazza Santa Trinità.
•0730-1200, 1600-1900. North of Ponte S Trinità on Via Tornabuoni.
*The elaborate 16thC Baroque facade by Buontalenti contrasts sharply with the serene simplicity of the 13thC Gothic interior. See* **A-Z**.

**SANTA MARIA DEL CARMINE** Piazza del Carmine.
•0900-1200, 1530-1830. Just west of S Spirito (see above).
*The original 13thC church was ravaged by fire in 1771 and only the sacristy, the Corsini Chapel and the Brancacci Chapel (see* ART 2*) have survived. See* **A-Z**.

**BADIA FIORENTINA** Via del Proconsolo.
•0800-1200, 1630-1830. Opposite the Bargello.
*Most notable for its fine tower, a splendid fresco by Filippino Lippi (see* **A-Z***) and sculptures by Mino da Fiesole. See* WALK 1, **A-Z**.

**SANTI APOSTOLI** Piazza del Limbo.
•1530-1830 Mon.-Sat., 0930-1230, 1530-1830 Sun. Near S Trinità.
*Houses Vasari's (see* **A-Z***) renowned* Immaculate Conception *(1541) and a terracotta tabernacle by della Robbia.*

**SANTA MARIA MADDALENA DEI PAZZI** Borgo Pinti 58.
•0900-1200, 1700-1900. Near the Piazza M. d'Azeglio.
*Named after a sainted member of the great Pazzi family whose remains lie in the beautiful choir chapel decorated by Silvani. See* ART 2.

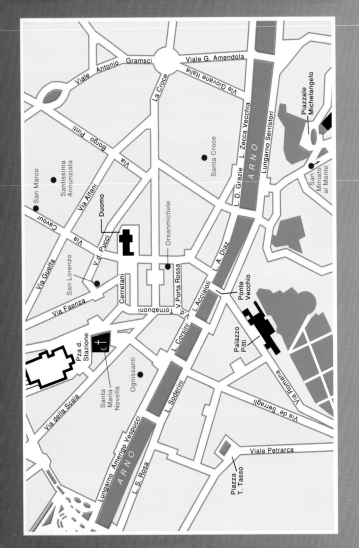

**SAN LORENZO** Piazza San Lorenzo.
•0700-1200, 1530-1900. 100 m south of the Mercato Centrale.
*The Medici family financed the rebuilding of this church to house their tombs. Visit the Sagrestia Vecchia decorated by Donatello. See* **WALK 2**, **A-Z**.

**SANTA CROCE** Piazza Santa Croce.
•0700-1230, 1500-1830. 100 m north of the Piazza Cavallari.
*Contains the tombs of famous Renaissance figures, including Michelangelo, Dante, Machiavelli and Galileo. See* **WALK 1**, **A-Z.**

**SANTA MARIA NOVELLA** Piazza Santa Maria Novella.
•0730-1145, 1530-1900. Opposite Central Station.
*13thC church with a fine Renaissance facade by Alberti. See* **WALK 2**, **A-Z**.

**OGNISSANTI** Piazza d'Ognissanti.
•0800-1200, 1600-1900. Along Borgognissanti from Piazza Goldoni.
*The refectory has splendid frescoes by Ghirlandaio and Botticelli. See* **A-Z**.

**ORSANMICHELE** Via dei Calzaioli.
•0800-1200, 1530-1830.
*Originally a grain market. The exterior is decorated with statues of the patron saints of the various merchants' guilds. See* **WALK 1**, **A-Z**.

**SANTISSIMA ANNUNZIATA** Piazza SS Annunziata.
•0700-1230, 1600-1900. At the end of the Via dei Servi.
*Contains a miraculous mural of* The Annunciation *supposedly painted by a monk and an angel. See* **A-Z**.

**SAN MINIATO AL MONTE** Monte alle Croci, Vle Galileo Galilei.
•0800-1215, 1500-1900. Near Piazzale Michelangelo. Bus 13.
*Attractive Romanesque church with a geometric facade of green and white marble embellished with a large 13thC mosaic. See* **WALK 3**, **A-Z**.

**SAN MARCO** Piazza San Marco.
•0700-1200 (0800-1315 Sun.), 1600-1930. North of the Battistero.
*Fra Angelico frescoes decorate the abbey cells. See* **MUSEUMS 1, WALK 2**, **A-Z**.

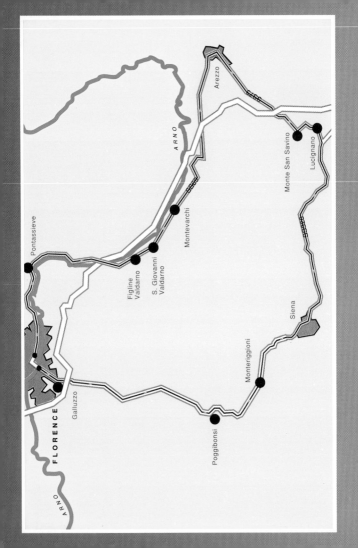

## Siena - Arezzo

**2 days -** *stopping overnight in Siena (book in advance at the tourist office in Florence - see* **Accommodation, Tourist Information***).*

Leave Florence by the Porta Romana (see **A-Z**) and head south towards Galluzzo (5 km) on the SS 2 (Via Cassia). On the right-hand side, just past the town, you will see an imposing hilltop monastery, the Certosa del Galluzzo (see **EXCURSION 3**). Soon after this you come to the *autostrada* (motorway) junction, where you should take the Siena turn-off onto the A 11, continuing until the Monteriggioni exit appears on your right.

**52 km - Monteriggioni.** This medieval fortified village, its circlet of walls and square towers crowning the top of the hill, was immortalized in Dante's *Inferno*. Park just outside the walls and take a walk or have a coffee in this quaint old village before rejoining the Siena road, then keep going until you see the exit for Siena Centro. Take this, and keep following similar signs until you also see signs for parking. Find a spot in one of the numerous car parks just outside the city walls, as the centre of the old town is closed to traffic.

**80 km - Siena** (see **A-Z**). Walk up to the huge fan or scallop-shaped main square, the famous Piazza del Campo, venue of the thrilling Palio horse race every July and August. Here you can visit the museum in the Gothic Palazzo Pubblico (0930-1930 Mon.-Sat., 0930-1330 Sun. & hol.; L. 5000) as well as its tall Torre del Mangia (102 m), which offers magnificent views over the city and surrounding countryside (1000-1800; tickets from first floor L. 3000). The 14thC Cappella di Piazza stands at its base. You will also find the tourist information office at No. 56. Leaving the *campo*, follow the signs (all Siena's chief monuments are signposted) for the Duomo, a stunning black and white marble structure containing a remarkable graffiti pavement executed by 40 different artists, and an octagonal pulpit by Nicola Pisano. The entrance to the charming Libreria Piccolominea lies to the left of the nave (0900-1915; L. 1500). The Museo dell'Opera del Duomo (Cathedral Museum) is housed in the Duomo Nuovo to the right of the cathedral (0900-1930; L. 4000). From here you can also reach the Battistero by a steep flight of steps. Going futher south onto the Via S Pietro, you will find the 15thC Palazzo Buonsignoria which houses the Pinacoteca,

containing 13th-16thC masterpieces belonging to the Sienese School of painting. You can also visit the Casa di Santa Caterina (north west of the *campo*, on the street of the same name), the birthplace of St Catherine, Italy's patron saint (her portrait hangs in the nearby basilica of San Domenico). Leave Siena on the SS 326 going in the direction of Arezzo. Turn left after 38 km and head north past the medieval village of Lucignano.

**131 km - Monte San Savino**. Walk round this Renaissance town, soaking in the atmosphere and admiring its many fine buildings. Look out in particular for the elegant Loggia dei Mercanti on the Corso Sangallo, which is attributed to local sculptor Andrea Sansovino (1467/70-1529). The grand Palazzo Comunale is on the same *corso*. Leave on the SS 73 going north east.

**172 km - Arezzo** (see **A-Z**). Follow the signs for the Piazza Grande. The square has a loggia designed by Vasari (see **A-Z**) which leads to the Palazzo Pretoria on its north-east side. The beautiful Pieve di S Maria backs onto the south-west side of the *piazza* while the Duomo and the house where Petrarch was born (Casa d. Petrarca) are to be found just north of the square. The church of S Francesco, further west in the centre of the old town (follow the signs), has a wonderful cycle of frescoes by Piero della Francesca, *The Legend of the True Cross*. Leave on the SS 69, following it along the left bank of the Arno past Montevarchi, S Giovanni Valdarno, Figline Valdarno and through the thriving wine town of Pontassieve until you get to Florence (85 km).

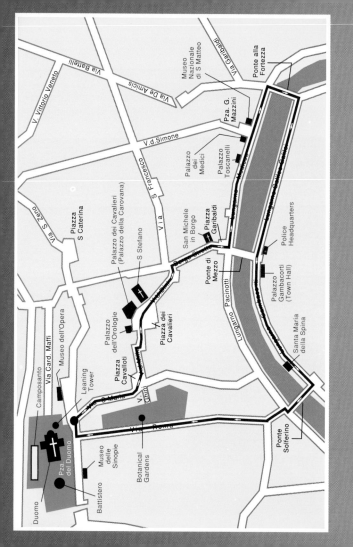

## Pisa

**1 day** - *91 km west of Florence on the A 11 motorway. SITA bus from behind the station or train to Pisa Station (1 hr).*

Begin your tour of Pisa at the Piazza del Duomo (or Campo dei Miracoli) north west of the town centre, site of Pisa's most famous building, the celebrated Torre Pendente or Leaning Tower of Pisa (0900-1800; L. 5000). The reason for the campanile's slant lies in the nature of the alluvial subsoil into which it began to sink during its construction in 1174. Architecturally, it is a perfect example of Pisan-Romanesque style. Opposite is the spectacular Duomo (begun 1064), similarly clad in horizontal stripes of black and white marble, which was financed by plunder from the Crusades (open 0745-1300, 1500-1730). The three sets of handsome bronze doors are by Bonanno Pisano (1180). The equally magnificent cruciform interior, with its splendid ceiling, boasts a beautiful (reconstructed) pulpit by Giovanni Pisano (1302-11), Galileo's Lamp, the oscillations of which were supposed to have helped Pisa University's famous professor develop his theories of pendular motion, and works by Cimabue (see **A-Z**), Ghirlandaio (see **A-Z**) and Andrea del Sarto, among many others. The Romanesque Battistero (begun 1153) facing the Duomo's west facade has a Gothic dome and arches, and houses a splendid pulpit by Nicola Pisano (his earliest known work). Nicola's father, Giovanni Pisano, sculpted the expressive figures which once adorned the entrance and are now housed in the town's National Museum (see below). The Camposanto (the cemetery) to the right is supposed to contain earth brought from Palestine during the Crusades (open 0900-1800). Monuments and sculptures belonging to this huge rectangular cloister suffered much war damage and its frescoes were removed for restoration. They can now be seen in the Museo delle Sinopie on the south side of the *piazza* behind the souvenir stalls; while treasures from the cathedral are housed in the Museo dell'Opera del Duomo (0900-1900 summer, 0900-1700 winter; closed 1 May, 25 Dec.; L. 4000) across from the tower.

Leaving the *piazza*, take the Via Santa Maria (off the south-eastern side near the tower) into the Piazza Cavalloti. Cross the square and take the Via dei Mille on the other side, which leads into the Piazza dei

Cavalieri through the Via Corsica. This *piazza*, its impressive graffiti-decorated 16thC *palazzo* (now a school) and the church of S Stefano are all named after the Knights of St Stephen, founded by Cosimo I. The Palazzo dell'Orologio, on the left of the Palazzo dei Cavalieri, reputedly stands on the remains of the infamous Torre della Fame where Count Ugolino della Gherardesca and his children were imprisoned and starved to death (the story figures in Canto 33 of Dante's *Inferno*). Take the small Via U. Dini to the right of the church and then turn first right into the Borgo Stretto. Continue along the *borgo* past the church of San Michele in Borgo (on your left) and cross the Piazza Garibaldi to the river.

Turn left onto the Lungarno Mediceo and stroll past the Palazzo Toscanelli (where Byron wrote *Don Juan*) to the little Piazza G. Mazzini where you will find the Palazzo dei Medici (now the Prefecture) and the Museo Nazionale di S Matteo (0830-1930 Tues.-Sun., closed 1 May, 15 Aug.; L. 3000). Continue along the Lungarno until you reach the Ponte alla Fortezza, then cross the river and turn right along the Lungarno Galileo Galilei. Just before the Ponte di Mezzo, on the left, you will see the police headquarters with its loggia and clock tower. Just after it is the Palazzo Gambacorti (now the Town Hall). Keep going until you reach the ornate little church of Santa Maria della Spina on the bank of the river (named after the holy relic it houses - a thorn from Christ's crown). Cross over the river again at the Ponte Solferino and follow the Via Roma (on the other side of the Piazza Solferino) past the Botanical Gardens (entrance at Via Luca Ghini 5; 0800-1230, 1430-1700 Mon.-Fri.) back to the Piazza del Duomo.

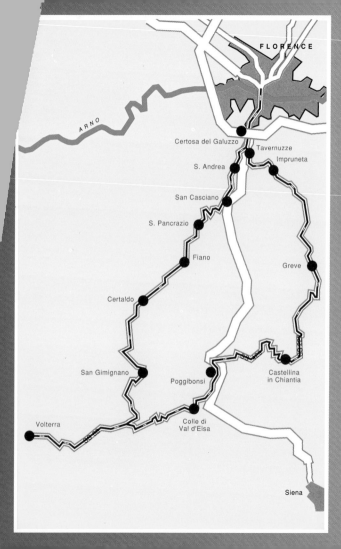

## Certaldo - Volterra

**1 day** - *leaving early and returning late.*

Leave Florence by the Siena road and pass through the town of
Galuzzo before turning off to the right and driving up to the monastery
(see **EXCURSION 1**).

**6 km - Certosa del Galuzzo**. An imposing 14thC Carthusian monastery
(also known as the Certosa di Val d'Ema). The Cistercian monks who
now occupy it hold conducted tours of the church, convent buildings
and the Gothic Palazzo degli Studi which houses an art gallery (hourly
0900-1200, 1600-1900 summer; 0900-1200, 1500-1700 winter). There
is also a shop selling alcoholic remedies distilled by the monks. Return
to the Siena road (Via Cassia) and carry on to the *autostrada* junction.
Head for Tavernuzze and turn right after 4.5 km.

**13 km - San Andrea in Percussina**. A picturesque hamlet with a *cantina*
(wine shop) and quaint well. You can see the Villa Serristori, better
known as the Albergaccio di Machiavelli, where Machiavelli (see **A-Z**)
once stayed. Continue on to San Casciano in Val di Pesa and then take
the south-west road passing through S Pancrazio, Faino, *etc*, until you
come to Certaldo where you should follow the signs for Certaldo Alto.
Park outside the walls of the old town.

**37 km - Certaldo Alto**. Time seems to have stood still in this medieval
town where Boccaccio (see **A-Z**), famous author of *The Decameron*,
lived and died. You can visit the Casa del Boccaccio at Via Boccaccio
18, a faithful reconstruction of his house (destroyed in WW II) which
now houses a library containing books on and by him. The 13thC
church of SS Jacopo e Filippo next door contains his tomb (in the
centre of the nave) as well as that of the Blessed Julia of Certaldo. The
stately Palazzo Pretorio at the end of the road contains a small Etruscan
museum and permanent exhibition of works inspired by the author, as
well as interesting 15th-16thC frescoes (0900-1230, 1500-1900
Tues.-Sun.).

**50 km - San Gimignano**. This medieval hill town is famous for its towers, which rise above the central (triangular) Piazza della Cisterna and
the Piazza del Duomo. The latter square is surrounded by impressive
public buildings, including the Collegiata, the ancient Palazzo del
Podestà and the 13thC Palazzo del Popolo, with its museum and art

gallery (0930-1230, 1530-1830 summer; 1000-1300, 1430-1730 winter; includes admission to chapel of S Fina) and Torre Grossa. The church of S Agostino in the northern part of the town contains a magnificent series of 14th-15thC frescoes depicting *The Life of St Augustine* by Gozzoli. Continue south west past Castelvecchio.

**79 km - Volterra.** Vestiges of this 2000 year-old town's Etruscan heritage can be seen in the town walls, the Porta all'Arco (southern Arch Gateway), the Porta Diana (Diana Gateway) and the ancient acropolis on the summit of the hill, while remains from the Roman period include the Roman Theatre (west of the Via Guarnacci) and Baths (in the area of the acropolis near the 500-year-old Medici Fortress). Fine collections of artefacts from these periods, as well as from the Villanovan Age, can be seen in the local Museo Etrusca Guarnacci on the Via Bon Minzoni. The beautiful Piazza dei Priori dates from medieval times and is dominated by the Palazzo dei Priori which houses a picture gallery containing several famous works. Facing the Priors' Palace is the Pretorian Palace with its tall tower commonly known as the Tower of the Piglet after the animal figure hanging on the facade. The Duomo and Battistero stand in the Piazza S Giovanni at the back of the Palazzo dei Priori; while the Museo d'Arte Sacra (Museum of Sacred Art) can be found in the neighbouring Via Roma. Alabaster is the town speciality and you will find articles made from this material for sale in many of the shops, as well as reproductions of the unusual Etruscan bronze figure known as *Evening Shadow*. Having bought your souvenirs, follow the SS 68 for 31 km to Colle Val d'Elsa. Join the *autostrada* just after the town and follow it north for 6 km before taking the Poggibonsi turn-off and following the signs for Castellina in Chianti on the SS 429. Continue north from Castellina along the SS 222, known as the Chiantigiana, through the fertile wine and olive-growing area of Chianti, passing through Greve on the way (19 km).

**172 km - Impruneta.** This well-known pottery centre (the clay for terracotta comes from here) is also famous for its huge annual agricultural fair (Oct.), its lively grape festival and its straw hats. Visit the Collegiata of Santa Maria dell'Impruneta before returning to Florence via Tavarnuzze (17 km).

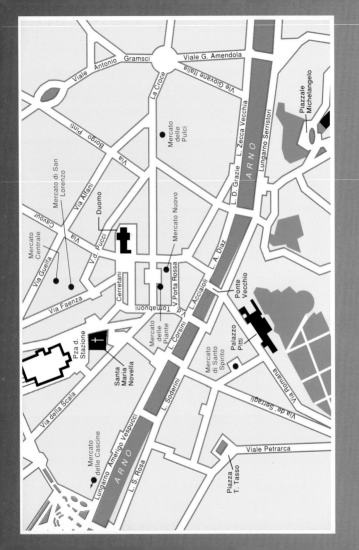

**MERCATO NUOVO** Piazza del Mercato Nuovo.
• 0900-1700 (summer), 0900-1800 Tues.-Sat. (winter). On Via Calimala.
*Familiarly known as Il Porcellino after the bronze statue of a boar erected here in 1612. Famous for straw goods, but you can also obtain other hand-crafted articles.*

**MERCATO DELLE PULCI** Piazza dei Ciompi.
• 0800-1300, 1530-1900 Tues.- Sat., 1000-1900 last Sun. of the month. North of Santa Croce on the Borgo Allegri.
*It's difficult to find real bargains in the flea market, but you should enjoy browsing amongst the old postcards, prints and other curiosities. The monthly market, with additional stalls in the surrounding streets, is best.*

**MERCATO DI SAN LORENZO** Via dell'Ariento & Piazza S Lorenzo.
• 0830-1900 Mon.-Sat. Extends north west of S Lorenzo.
*Florence's busy central market is a bit of a tourist trap as you may find similar goods (leather jackets, shoes, etc ) are cheaper in the shops. See* **WALK 2**.

**MERCATO DELLE PIANTE** Piazza della Repubblica.
• 0800-1700 Thurs. Between Duomo and Ponte Vecchio along Via Roma.
*Delightful weekly flower market in the loggia of the main post office.*

**MERCATO DELLE CASCINE** Pza Vittorio & Pza di Porta al Prato.
• 0700-1300 Tues. Bordering the river in the Cascine Park.
*A charming open-air market selling fresh produce, household goods and clothing. The cheapest market in town.*

**MERCATO CENTRALE** Piazza del Mercato Centrale.
• 0700-1400 (and 1600-2000 Sat.) Mon.-Sat. (15 Sept.-15 June).
*Central food market, housed in a huge 19thC cast-iron edifice, offering fresh produce at reasonable prices. Go early to experience the morning bustle.*

**MERCATO DI SANTO SPIRITO** Piazza Santo Spirito.
• 0700-1300 Mon.-Sat. Left bank of the Arno beyond Ponte S Trinità.
*This lively little food market on the charming Piazza S Spirito also sells wooden articles, crafted locally, and second-hand goods.*

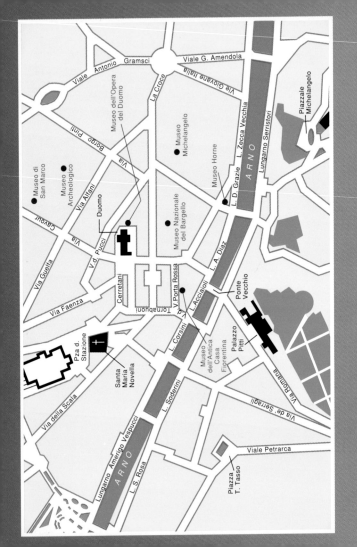

**MUSEO NAZIONALE DEL BARGELLO** Via del Proconsolo 4.
•0900-1400 Tues.-Sat., 0900-1300 Sun. & hol. •L. 3000.
*Contains one of the world's finest collections of sculpture, with particular emphasis on 14th-17thC Tuscan pieces. See* PALAZZI 1, WALK 1, **Bargello.**

**MUSEO DELL'OPERA DEL DUOMO** Piazza del Duomo 9.
•0900-1930 (1700 winter) Mon.-Sat., 1000-1230 Sun. (free). •L. 3000.
*Sculptures from the Duomo (see* CHURCHES 1, WALK 1, **A-Z**) *and Battistero (see* WALK 1, **A-Z**). *See* **A-Z**.

**MUSEO DI SAN MARCO** Piazza San Marco 1.
•0900-1400 Tues.-Sat., 0900-1300 Sun. •L. 3000.
*Known as the Fra Angelico Museum after the Dominican monk whose fine frescoes decorate the monastery where he lived. See* CHURCHES 2, **San Marco**.

**MUSEO MICHELANGELO (CASA BUONARROTI)**
Via Ghibellina 70.
•0930-1330 Wed.-Mon. •Free.
*Most notable for the fine collection of drawings and sculptures by the great master, assembled by his grand-nephew. See* **Michelangelo**, **A-Z**.

**MUSEO HORNE** Via dei Benci 6.
•1600-2000 Mon.-Fri., 0900-1300 Sat. Near Santa Croce. •L. 3000.
*Giotto's painting of St Stephen is one of the main attractions in this private collection donated to the city by the art historian Herbert Percy Horne.*

**MUSEO DELL'ANTICA CASA FIORENTINA** Via Porta Rossa 13.
•0900-1400 Tues.-Sat., 0900-1300 Sun. Pza S Trinità bus stop. •L. 2000.
*Housed in the Palazzo Davanzati (see* PALAZZI 1), *the museum illustrates the way of life of a wealthy Florentine family of the 14thC. The beautiful Sala dei Papagalli (Parrot Room) is particularly noteworthy.*

**MUSEO ARCHEOLOGICO** Via della Colonna 38.
•0900-1400 Tues.-Sat., 0900-1300 Sun. & hol. •L. 3000.
*On three floors of the beautiful 17thC Palazzo della Crocetta. Interesting collection of Etruscan remains, classical statues and ancient Egyptian finds.*

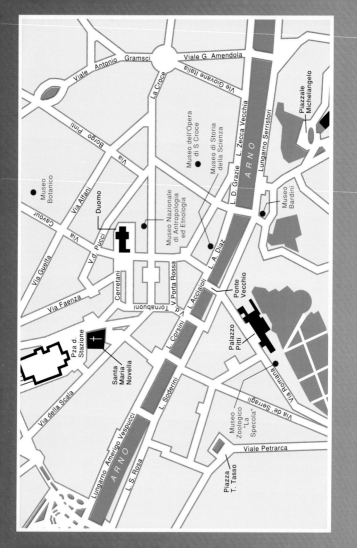

## MUSEO DELL'OPERA DI S CROCE (MUSEO CIMABUE)
Piazza Santa Croce 16.
● 0900-1230, 1500-1830 (1700 winter) Thurs.-Tues. ● L. 2000.
*Cimabue's painted Crucifix can be found in the old monastery refectory along with Gaddi's fresco of The Last Supper. See* WALK 1, **Santa Croce**.

## MUSEO BARDINI Piazza de' Mozzi 1.
● 0900-1400 Mon.-Sat., 0800-1300 Sun. & hol. South of the Ponte alle Grazie. ● L. 2000.
*A vast and wildly eclectic private collection which defies proper classification. See* **A-Z**.

## MUSEO DI STORIA DELLA SCIENZA Piazza dei Giudici 1.
● 0930-1300 Mon.-Sat. (and 1400-1700 Mon., Wed., Fri.). On the Lungarno Medici. ● L. 5000.
*Exhibits early scientific instruments from the grand-ducal collections and the hospital of Santa Maria Nuova. Look out for Galileo's telescope. See* **A-Z**.

## MUSEO NAZIONALE DI ANTROPOLOGIA ED ETNOLOGIA
Via del Proconsolo 12.
● 0900-1300 Thurs., Fri., Sat., 3rd Sun. of the month. ● Free.
*This museum (founded 1869), located on the ground and first floors of the Palazzo Nonfinito, traces the early history of man and has displays covering customs and costumes from around the world. See* WALK 1.

## MUSEO ZOOLOGICO 'LA SPECOLA' Via Romana 17.
● 0900-1200 Mon., Tues.-Sat., 0930-1230 2nd Sun. of the month. Near the Palazzo Pitti. ● Free.
*Apart from a wide range of specimens, the museum boasts a remarkable collection of some 600 anatomical models in coloured wax.*

## MUSEO BOTANICO Via G. La Pira 4 (entrance at Via Micheli 3).
● 0900-1200 Mon., Wed., Fri. Second floor of the Institute of Botany.
● Free.
*Contains one of the largest herbariums in the world, a fine display of wax models of plants, and a rare 15thC illustrated manuscript.*

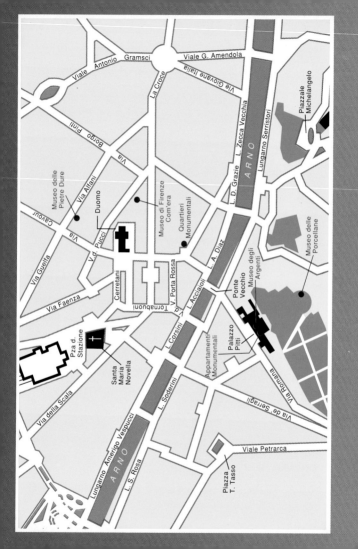

**MUSEO DELLE PIETRE DURE** Via degli Alfani 78.
•0900-1400 Mon.-Sat (closed hol.). Near the Accademia. •L. 2000.
*A small museum, next to the workshop which supplied the Cappelle Medicee (see* **WALK 2**, **A-Z***), rich in examples of semi-precious stone inlay.*

**MUSEO DI FIRENZE COM'ERA** Via dell'Oriuolo 24.
•0900-1400 Mon.-Wed., Fri., Sat., 0800-1300 Sun. & hol.
West of the Duomo. •Free.
*Exhibits of old photographs, postcards, maps, architectural plans, engravings and etchings tracing Florence's development from the 15thC.*

**MUSEO DELLE PORCELLANE** Giardino di Boboli.
•0900-1400 Tues.-Sat., 0900-1300 Sun. •L. 4000 (includes admission to the Museo dei Costumi and the Museo degli Argenti - see below).
*Exquisite selection of European porcelain from the collections of the Medicis (see* **A-Z***) and the grand dukes of Lorraine and Savoy. See* **Giardino di Boboli***.*

**MUSEO DEGLI ARGENTI** Palazzo Pitti.
•0900-1400 Tues.-Sat., 0900-1300 Sun. Entrance to left of courtyard.
•L. 4000 (includes admission to the Museo dei Costumi and the Museo delle Porcellane - see above).
*The glittering treasures of the Medicis and the House of Lorraine. See the fabulous collection of antique vases. See* **PALAZZI 1**, **WALK 1**, **Palazzo Pitti***.*

**QUARTIERI MONUMENTALI** Palazzo Vecchio, Piazza d. Signoria.
•0900-1900 Mon.-Fri., 0800-1300 Sun. & hol. Entrance in courtyard.
•L. 4000.
*The grandiose Sala dei Cinquecento by Cronaca contains Michelangelo's (see* **A-Z***) The Genius of Victory. See* **PALAZZI 1**, **WALK 1**, **Palazzo Vecchio***.*

**APPARTAMENTI MONUMENTALI** Palazzo Pitti.
•0900-1400 Tues.-Sat., 0900-1300 Sun. •L. 4000 (includes admission to the Galleria Palatina - see **ART 1**).
*Opulent state apartments containing numerous portraits of the Medicis (see* **A-Z***) who once occupied the palace. See* **PALAZZI 1**, **WALK 1**, **Palazzo Pitti***.*

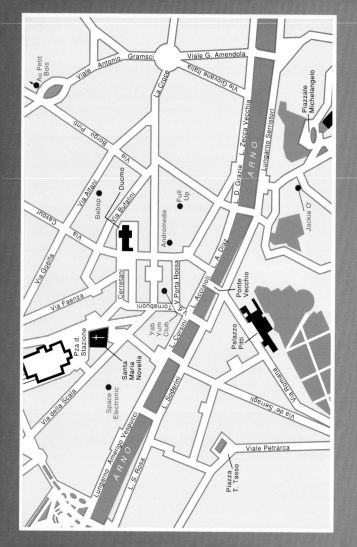

**JACKIE O'** Via dell'Erta Canina 24b.
- 2200-0300 Mon.-Sat. West of the Piazzale Michelangelo.
- L. 20,000 Mon.-Thurs., L. 25,000 Fri., Sat.

*This excellent disco is one of the largest in Florence. Plays the latest sounds and is popular with fashionable young professionals.*

**YAB YUM CLUB** Via Sassetti 5r.
- 1000-0400. Take the Via Strozzi from the Piazza della Repubblica.
- L. 20,000 (includes first drink).

*The trendiest club in town.*

**FULL UP** Via della Vigna Vecchia 21r.
- 2200-0300 Wed.-Mon. (closed mid-July to end Aug.). Near the Bargello. • L. 20,000 (includes first drink; second drink L. 10,000 at bar).

*Crowded, fashionable disco with interesting decor.*

**SPACE ELECTRONIC** Via Palazzuolo 37.
- 0930-0300. Behind Ognissanti. • L. 10,000 (includes first drink).

*Florence's largest and most popular disco, equipped with two dance floors, videos, and great rock music in a way-out setting.*

**BEBOP** Via dei Servi.
- 1000-0400. Between the Duomo and SS Annuziata. • L. 15,000.

*Sophisticated jazz club with live performances.*

**ANDROMEDA** Via Cimatori 13.
- 2200-0300 Tues.-Sun. (closed Aug.). Behind the Piazza della Signoria.
- L. 15,000 (includes first drink).

*This disco in the heart of the Centro Storico has two dance floors and great laser effects. The Sunday floor shows are a special attraction.*

**AU PETIT BOIS** Via Ferrucci, Fiesole.
- 2200-0300. 500 m along road to Olga. • L. 13,000 Mon.-Sat., L. 15,000 Sun. (includes first drink).

*This spacious nightclub in the hills of Fiesole has an elegant piano bar, a discotheque, and an open-air dance floor in summer.*

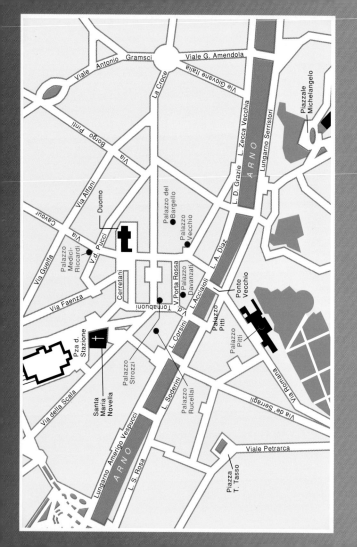

**PALAZZO PITTI** Piazza Pitti.
*Built by the wealthy merchant Luca Pitti, the facade of this impressive palace is over 200 m long. Today it contains numerous galleries and museums. See* **ART 1, MUSEUMS 3, WALK 1, A-Z.**

**PALAZZO MEDICI-RICCARDI** Via Cavour 1.
•0900-1200, 1500-1645 Mon.-Sat. (closed hol.).
*Home of the Medicis (see* **A-Z***) until 1540. Now houses the Prefecture. See the Cappella B. Gozzoli and the Museo Mediciana. See* **ART 2, WALK 2, A-Z.**

**PALAZZO DAVANZATI** Porta Rossa 9.
Piazza Santa Trinità bus stop.
*Built in the 14thC by one of Florence's oldest, most influential merchant families. Contains the Museo dell'Antica Casa Fiorentina (see* **MUSEUMS 1***).*

**PALAZZO VECCHIO (DELLA SIGNORIA)** Piazza Signoria.
•0900-1900 Mon.-Fri., 0900-1300 Sun.
*Became known as the Old Palace when the Medici ducal residence moved to the Palazzo Pitti. Now it is the Town Hall. See* **MUSEUMS 3, WALK 1, A-Z.**

**PALAZZO STROZZI** Via Tornabuoni.
•Open for exhibitions only.
*Largest 15thC palace in Florence, reflecting the wealth and status of its owner Filippo Strozzi, major rival of the Medicis (see* **A-Z***). A small museum illustrates the palace's history (open 1600-1900 Mon., Wed., Fri.). See* **A-Z.**

**PALAZZO RUCELLAI** Via della Vigna Nuova 18.
•Open by request only. Between Piazza Goldoni and Via Tornabuoni.
*One of the most pleasing and influential pieces of architecture in the city. Attributed to Alberti, it was built by Rossellino (c.1446-51) for Giovanni Rucellai, one of Florence's rich merchants and an ally of the Medicis.*

**PALAZZO DEL BARGELLO** Via del Proconsolo 4.
*The medieval residence of the Podestà, the city's governing magistrates, before becoming the police headquarters and a prison. Now it houses the National Sculpture Museum. See* **MUSEUMS 1, WALK 1, Bargello.**

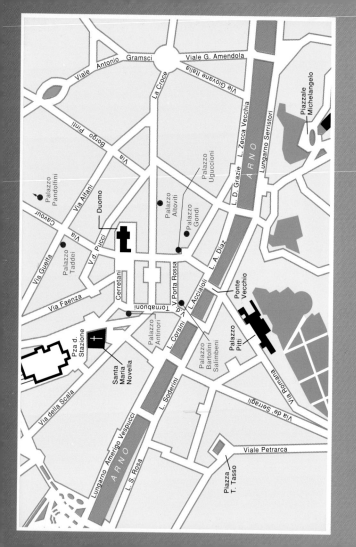

**PALAZZO ANTINORI** Piazza Antinori.
•Admittance to *cantinetta* only. North end of the Via Tornabuoni.
*Built by Giuliano da Maiano (c.1495) for the wine-growing Boni family.*
*Features an attractive interior garden and a cantinetta (wine cellar and bar).*

**PALAZZO BARTOLINI-SALIMBENI** Piazza Santa Trinità 1.
•No admittance.
*Classical palace with Romanesque windows by d'Agnolo (1517-20), who*
*was severely criticized for its ecclesiastical appearance. The architect's*
*retort above the door reads: 'It is easier to criticize than to imitate'.*

**PALAZZO PANDOLFINI** Via San Gallo 74.
•No admittance. Between the Piazza della Libertà and San Marco.
*Commissioned by the Archbishop of Troia, designed by Raphael and probably*
*built by the Sangallo brothers (c.1520). Note the magnificent cornice.*

**PALAZZO GONDI** Piazza San Firenze 2.
•No admittance. Opposite the Palazzo Vecchio.
*Beautiful Renaissance palace constructed by Giuliano da Sangallo (c.1490).*
*Visit the delightful courtyard and fountain by applying to the caretaker.*

**PALAZZO TADDEI** Via de' Ginori 17-21.
•No admittance. North east of the Piazza S Lorenzo.
*Typical 16thC palace built by Baccio d'Agnolo for another of Florence's*
*affluent merchants. Raphael stayed here in 1505.*

**PALAZZO UGUCCIONI** Piazza della Signoria 7.
•No admittance. Opposite the Palazzo Vecchio.
*Built in 1549 from plans supposedly sent by Michelangelo (see **A-Z**) from*
*Rome. Note the attractive facade, attributed to Mariotto di Zanobi, and the*
*bust of Francesco I looking down from the first-floor balcony.*

**PALAZZO ALTOVITI** Borgo degli Albizzi 18.
•No admittance. Behind the Bargello.
*Also known as the Palazzo dei Visacci (Palace of Ugly Faces) after the*
*marble busts of prominent Florentine figures which adorn the facade.*

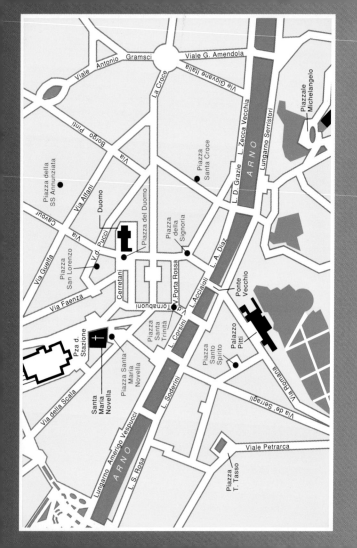

**PIAZZA DEL DUOMO** Centre of the old city.
*The splendour of the Duomo (see* **CHURCHES 1**, **A-Z**)*, the octagonal elegance of the Battistero (see* **A-Z**) *and the grace of the Campanile make this the most beautiful square in Florence. See* **WALK 1***.*

**PIAZZA DELLA SIGNORIA** Take Via de' Calzaioli from Duomo.
*Historical and political heart of the city, dominated by the Palazzo Vecchio (see* **PALAZZI 1**, **A-Z**)*. Savonarola was executed here. See* **WALK 1**, **A-Z***.*

**PIAZZA DELLA SS ANNUNZIATA** North end of the Via dei Servi.
*Beautifully proportioned square bordered by elegant porticoes and the 16thC Palazzo Riccardi-Mannelli. Features two bronze fountains (1629) and an equestrian statue of Grand Duke Ferdinando I. See* **CHURCHES 2**, **A-Z***.*

**PIAZZA SANTA TRINITÀ** Near the Ponte S Trinità.
*A column bearing a bronze statue of Justice (1581) stands at the centre of the square. It is bordered by the Baroque church of S Trinità (see* **CHURCHES 1**, **A-Z**) *and the Palazzo Bartolini-Salimbeni (see* **PALAZZI 2**)*.*

**PIAZZA SAN LORENZO** 150 m north of the Battistero.
*One of the liveliest market squares in Florence (see* **MARKETS**)*. Site of the church of San Lorenzo (see* **CHURCHES 2**, **WALK 2**, **A-Z**)*.*

**PIAZZA SANTA CROCE** East of Piazza della Signoria.
*Large rectangular square fronting the medieval church of Santa Croce (see* **CHURCHES 2**, **A-Z**)*. The former site of popular preaching, rowdy political gatherings, book burnings, executions, football games and jousts put on by the Medici (see* **A-Z**) *grand dukes. See* **WALK 1**, **Events***.*

**PIAZZA SANTA MARIA NOVELLA** Near Central Station.
*Popular medieval meeting-place, overlooked by the magnificent facade of Santa Maria Novella (see* **CHURCHES 2**, **A-Z**)*. See* **WALK 2***.*

**PIAZZA SANTO SPIRITO** Across the Arno from Santa Trinità.
*A busy market (see* **MARKETS**)*, shady garden and stately church (see* **CHURCHES 1**, **Santo Spirito**) *make this one of the city's most charming squares.*

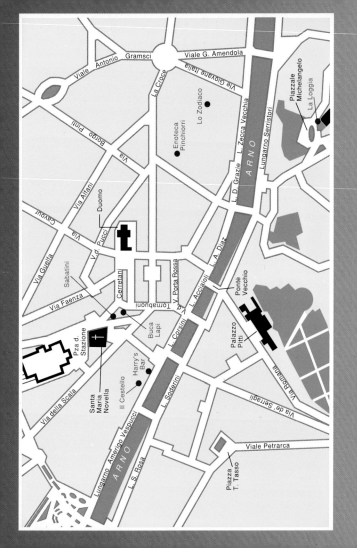

## Expensive

**ENOTECA PINCHIORRI** Via Ghibellina 87.
- 1230-1400, 1930-2200 Tues.-Sat.; 1930-2200 Mon. (closed Aug. and Christmas). Near Santa Croce. •**From** L. 90,000-100,000.
*Creative Franco-Florentine cuisine accompanied by a first-rate selection of fine wines. Famous throughout Italy and fabulously expensive. Book in advance (tel: 242777).*

**IL CESTELLO** Hotel Excelsior, Piazza Ognissanti 3.
- 1200-1500, 1900-2330. •From L. 50,000.
*An elegant rooftop (mid-May to Sept. - otherwise on ground floor) restaurant serving a wide range of excellent 'international' dishes as well as traditional cuisine. Lobster, truffles or the local ribollita (thick soup) are all good choices.*

**LO ZODIACO** Via delle Casine 2.
- 1200-1500, 1930-0100 Mon.-Sat. Behind S Croce. •From L. 50,000.
*Seafood restaurant with an excellent menu. Try their green pepper spannoc-chie (large shrimps). Book in advance (tel: 2340834/2340984).*

**HARRY'S BAR** Lungarno Vespucci 22r.
- 1130-1600, 1730-2400 Mon.-Sat. (closed part of Aug., Nov. & Dec.). Near Ognissanti. •From L. 55,000.
*Favourite meeting place of English-speaking visitors. Overpriced, but tasteful.*

**SABATINI** Via Panzani 9A.
- 1200-1430, 1930-2230 Tues.-Sun. Near S M. Novella. •From L. 70,000.
*Regional specialities and the best bistecca alla fiorentina (see **Food**) in town.*

**LA LOGGIA** Piazzale Michelangelo 1r.
- 1200-1430 (last orders), 1915-2230 (last orders) Thurs.-Tues. (closed Aug.). •From L. 50,000.
*Breathtaking panorama of the city from the terrace. Classic Italian dishes.*

**BUCA LAPI** Via del Trebbio 1r.
- 1230-1430, 1930-2230 Tues.-Sat.; 1930-2230 Mon. •From L. 50,000.
*Enjoy 'international' or Tuscan dishes in a cheerful atmosphere. The steaks are particularly good.*

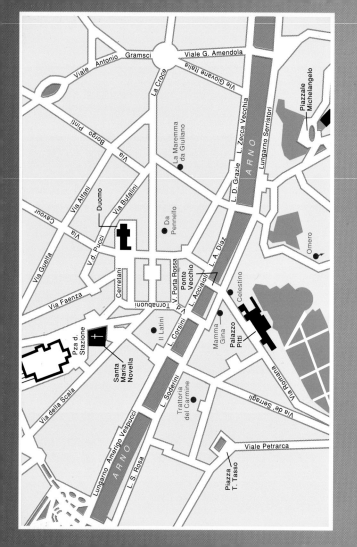

## Medium

**LA MAREMMA DA GIULIANO** Via Verdi 16r.
• 1200-1500, 1900-2300 Mon., Tues., Thurs.-Sat.; 1200-1500 Sun.
Near Santa Croce. •L. 35,000-50,000.
*Serves delicious Tuscan dishes, especially from the coastal region of Maremma. The pappardelle alla lepre (pasta with hare) is recommended.*

**OMERO** Via del Pian dei Giullari 11r, Arcetri.
• 1200-1430, 1930-2230 Wed.-Mon. (closed Aug.). •L. 30,000-50,000.
*Hillside restaurant serving huge portions of good Tuscan food. A popular spot for Sunday lunch. Book in advance for a table with a view (tel: 220053).*

**CELESTINO** Piazza Santa Felicità 4r.
• 1130-1500, 1900-2300 Mon.-Sat. (closed Aug., end of Dec.). Near the Ponte Vecchio. •L. 35,000-40,000.
*Popular little trattoria with plenty of atmosphere and fast service.*

**IL LATINI** Via Palchetti 6r.
• 1230-1430, 1900-2230 Wed.-Sun.; 1900-2230 Tues. (closed mid-July to mid-Aug., 23 Dec.-6 Jan.). Behind Palazzo Rucellai. •L. 30,000-50,000.
*Typically noisy, friendly trattoria - very authentic, but definitely not relaxing.*

**MAMMA GINA** Borgo San Jacopo 37r.
• 1200-1430, 1900-2230 Mon.-Sat. (closed 6-20 Aug.). Between Ponte Vecchio and S Spirito on the left bank of the Arno. •L. 40,000-45,000.
*Popular with those wanting a simple menu of authentic local dishes.*

**TRATTORIA DEL CARMINE** Piazza del Carmine 18.
• 1200-1445, 1900-2200 Mon.-Sat. (closed Sat. in summer, Aug.). On the left bank of the Arno. •L. 30,000-35,000.
*Typical trattoria offering a large selection of home-made desserts. Eat outdoors in summer and enjoy the view of the piazza.*

**DA PENNELLO** Via Dante Alighieri 4r.
• 1200-1430, 1900-2200 Tues.-Sun. lunchtime (closed Aug.). Near the Piazza della Signoria. •L. 30,000-35,000.
*Offers a wide range of typical dishes. Enjoy the friendly atmosphere.*

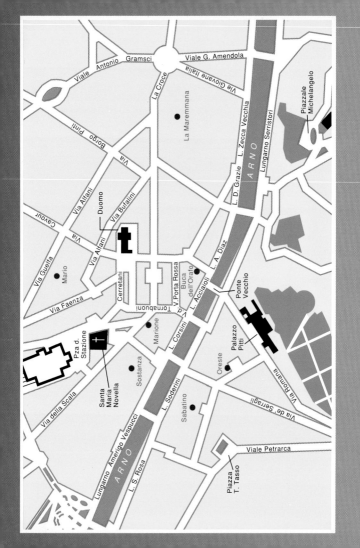

## Budget

**SOSTANZA ('IL TROIA')** Via del Porcellana 25r.
• 1200-1410 (last orders), 1930-2130 (last orders) Mon.-Fri. (closed
hol.). Near Ognissanti. • L. 25,000-30,000.
*Typical trattoria (nicknamed 'The Whore'), where you literally rub shoulders
with your neighbour. Authentic Tuscan dishes and friendly service -
altogether excellent value.*

**BUCA DELL'ORAFO** Volta dei Girolami 28r.
• 1130-1500, 1930-2330 Tues.-Sat. Near the Ponte Vecchio.
• L. 25,000-30,000.
*It is essential to reserve a table in this small, popular trattoria. One of its
specialities is stracotto alla fiorentina (Florentine-style beef stew).*

**MARIONE** Via della Spada 27r.
• 1200-1430, 1930-2230 Mon.-Sat. Off the Via Tornabuoni.
• L. 18,000-25,000.
*Busy establishment with a good selection of simple local dishes at reasonable
prices. Usually frequented by locals, but also offers a cheap tourist menu.*

**MARIO** Via Rosina 2r.
• 1200-1430 Mon.-Sat. Behind Mercato di S Lorenzo. • L. 15,000-25,000.
*Lunch spot much frequented by locals and market people. The service is
simple and fast, the food typically Tuscan and the atmosphere friendly.*

**LA MAREMMANA** Via dei Macci 77r.
• 1230-1500, 1930-2230 Mon.-Sat. (closed Aug.). Beside the Mercato di
Sant'Ambrogio. • L. 14,000-30,000. Tourist menu from L. 14,000-21,000.
*Offers a large selection of meat and fish dishes and delicious antipasti.*

**ORESTE** Piazza Santo Spirito 16.
• 1200-1445, 1900-2230 Thurs.-Tues. lunchtime. • L. 18,000-25,000.
*Eat outside in the warm evening air and sample tasty traditional cuisine.*

**SABATINO** Borgo San Frediano 39r.
• 1200-1400, 1900-2200 Mon.-Fri. (closed Aug.). • L. 18,000-25,000.
*Family-run trattoria offering good, simple, home cooking at reasonable prices.*

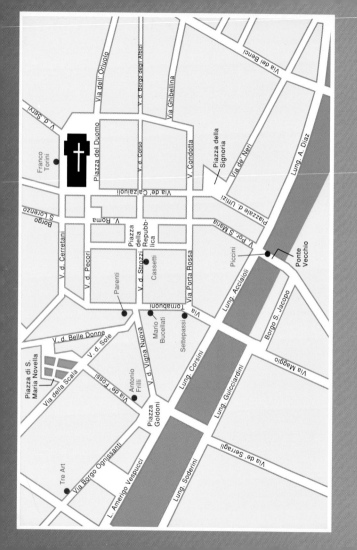

## Arts & Crafts

**MARIO BUCELLATI** Via Tornabuoni 71.
•0900-1300, 1600-1900 Tues.-Fri., Sat. am (summer), Mon. pm (winter).
*Reproductions of antique gold jewellery by this famous goldsmith.*

**PICCINI** Ponte Vecchio 21/23r.
•0900-1300, 1530-1930 Tues.-Sun.
*A small shop selling silver and gold items, jewellery, filigree and pietre dure mosaics. There is another branch in the Via Por Santa Maria.*

**FRANCO TORINI** Piazza del Duomo 10.
•0900-1300, 1600-1930 Mon.-Sat.
*One of the oldest jewellery shops in Florence, a family business selling delicate and original items.*

**SETTEPASSI** Via Tornabuoni 25r.
•0930-1300, 1500-1930 Tues.-Sat.
*Specializes in luxury pieces, both modern and traditional in style.*

**CASSETTI** Via degli Strozzi 7/9r.
•0900-1300, 1600-1900 Mon.-Sat.
*Famous throughout Tuscany for the exceptional quality of its silverware.*

**TRE ART** Borgognissanti 88r.
•0930-1300, 1530-1900 Tues.-Fri., Sat. am (summer),
Mon. pm (winter).
*Enticing display of delicate tableware, porcelain and glass (original designs).*

**ANTONIO FRILLI** Via de' Fossi 24-6r.
•0900-1930 Tues.-Fri., Sat. am (summer), Mon. pm (winter).
*Art studio specializing in marbles and bronzes, including fine reproductions.*

**PARENTI** Via Tornabuoni 93.
•0900-1300, 1530-1930 Tues.-Fri., Sat. am (summer),
Mon. pm (winter).
*A sort of luxury bazaar selling porcelain, glassware and curiosities as well as bags and accessories. An ideal place to browse for an unusual gift.*

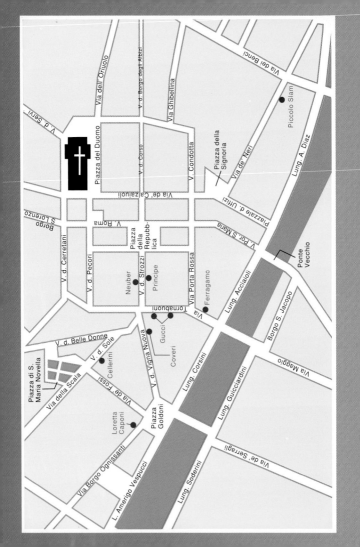

## Clothes

**LORETTA CAPONI** Borgognissanti 12.
•0930-1300, 1600-1900 Tues.-Fri., Sat. am (summer), Mon. pm (winter).
*Lingerie boutique with an exclusive range of hand-embroidered nightdresses.*

**GUCCI** Via Tornabuoni 57r-73/75r.
•0930-1300, 1530-1930 Mon.-Sat.
*Internationally-renowned boutique famous for its accessories as much as for its clothes. Even sells household goods under its famous label.*

**COVERI** Via della Vigna Nuova 27.
•0900-2000 (1930 winter) Tues.-Fri., Sat. am (summer), Mon. pm (winter).
*One of a national chain carrying a good selection of clothes and shoes.*

**PRINCIPE** Via Strozzi 21-9r.
•0930-1300, 1530-1930 (1600-2000 winter) Tues.-Fri., Sat. am (summer), Mon. pm (winter).
*Department store carrying a classical line in high-quality clothes.*

**FERRAGAMO** Via Tornabuoni 16.
•0930-1930 Tues.-Fri., Sat. am (summer), Mon. pm (winter).
*Chic male and female fashions. Branches worldwide.*

**PICCOLO SLAM** Via de' Neri 9, 11r.
•0930-1300, 1530-1930 Tues.-Sat. (summer), 1100-1300, 1600-2000 Tues.-Sat. (winter). South east of the Palazzo Vecchio.
*Cute children's clothes and trendy gear for teenagers.*

**CELLERINI** Via del Sole 37r.
•0930-1300, 1530-1930 Tues.-Fri., Sat. am (summer), Mon. pm (winter). Off the Via della Scalla in the direction of the Palazzo Strozzi.
*Exclusive leather shop specializing in crocodile and lizard-skin accessories.*

**NEUBER** Via Strozzi 32r.
•0930-1300, 1530-1930 Tues.-Sat., 1530-1930 Sun., Mon.
*Carries a classical line in top-quality clothes for all occasions.*

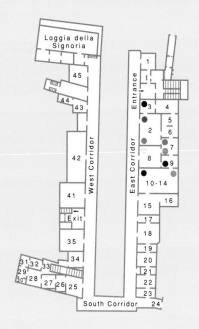

Loggia della Signoria

45

44
43

West Corridor

42

41

Exit

35

34

31 32 33
29
30 28 27 26 25

South Corridor

Entrance

East Corridor

1

3 4
2 5
6
7
8
9
10-14
15 16
17
18
19
20
21
22
23
24

● CIMABUE

● GIOTTO

● SIMONE MARTINI

● DOMENICO VENEZIANO

● UCCELLO

● LIPPI, FRA FILIPPO

● BOTTICELLI

● GOES, HUGO VAN DER

**CIMABUE** Room 2.
Madonna in Maestà, *formerly an altarpiece in S Trinità (see* **A-Z***), is a char-acteristically dramatic treatment of the subject by this artist. See* **A-Z**.

**GIOTTO** Room 2.
Virgin and Child with Angels and Saints *reveals Giotto's revolutionary con-cern with pictorial space, which broke with the Byzantine tradition and had such a profound influence on Western painting. See* **A-Z**.

**SIMONE MARTINI** Room 3.
*The large and richly-coloured* Annunciation, *painted in collaboration with Memmi (the artist's brother-in-law), is one of the finest examples of the Gothic-Sienese School of painting.*

**DOMENICO VENEZIANO** Room 7.
Madonna and Child with Four Saints *(c.1445), originally in S Lucia dei Magnoli, displays a sublime, and much imitated, use of light and perspective.*

**UCCELLO** Room 7.
*The magnificent* Battle of San Romano *(c.1455) was originally the central panel in a triptych painted for the Medici Palace. Although painted in an unnatural style, it reveals the artist's fascination with perspective. See* **A-Z**.

**LIPPI, FRA FILIPPO** Room 8.
*The best example of Lippi's paintings of the Madonna and Child is the* Madonna del Bambino e due Angeli *(1465). Its influence is clearly reflected in the works of Botticelli (see* **A-Z***), his pupil. See* **A-Z**.

**BOTTICELLI** Rooms 9, 10-14.
*Unique selection of Botticelli's early (Room 9) and later works (Rooms 10-14).* Primavera *and* Birth of Venus *(c.1482-4) are his most famous. See* **A-Z**.

**GOES, HUGO VAN DER** Room 14.
*The brilliant technique and spacial depth revealed in the Flemish artist's triptych of the* Adoration of the Shepherds *(c.1474-76) had a great and lasting effect on Florentine art.*

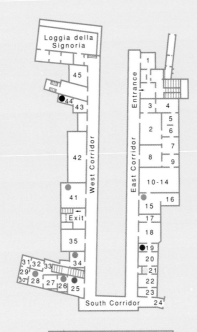

Loggia della Signoria

45

44

43

42 West Corridor

41

Exit

35

34

31 32 33

29 30 28 27 26 25

South Corridor

Entrance

1

3 4

2 5

6

7

8 9

East Corridor

10-14

16

15

17

18

19

20

21

22

23

24

● LEONARDO DA VINCI
● PERUGINO
○ BELLINI, GIOVANNI
● MICHELANGELO
● RAPHAEL
● TITIAN
● VERONESE
● RUBENS
● REMBRANDT

**LEONARDO DA VINCI** Room 15.
*Both Leonardo's drawing of* The Adoration of the Magi *(1481) and his* Annunciation *(1475) bear witness to his innovative genius. See* **A-Z***.*

**PERUGINO** Room 19.
*Among the splendid series of portraits by Perugino is an admirable study of* Francesco delle Opere.

**BELLINI, GIOVANNI** Room 21.
*Bellini's* Sacred Allegory *and* Lamentation of Christ *are fine examples of the wealth of Venetian art housed in this room.*

**MICHELANGELO** Room 25.
Holy Family *(1503) is the only painting by Michelangelo in Florence. The depth and solidity of the figures strongly reflect the artist's sculptural concerns. See* **A-Z***.*

**RAPHAEL** Room 26.
*A good range of paintings belonging to the artist's Florentine period including the* Madonna of the Goldfinch *(1506) and* Leo X and Cardinals *(1519).*

**TITIAN** Room 28.
*Titian's famous nude* Venus of Urbino *(1538) is imbued with a sensuality and expressive use of colour typical of the great master.*

**VERONESE** Room 34.
*A sumptuous use of colour and light characterize* The Holy Family and St Barbara *and* The Annunciation, *both fine examples of 16thC Venetian art.*

**RUBENS** Room 41.
*The portrait of Rubens' wife* Isabella Brandt *shows great tenderness, while the* Entry of Henry IV into Paris *reveals his ease in handling historical themes.*

**REMBRANDT** Room 44.
*Two of the Dutch painter's famous self-portraits are here as well as* Portrait of an Old Man *(1664), considered to be one of his best works.*

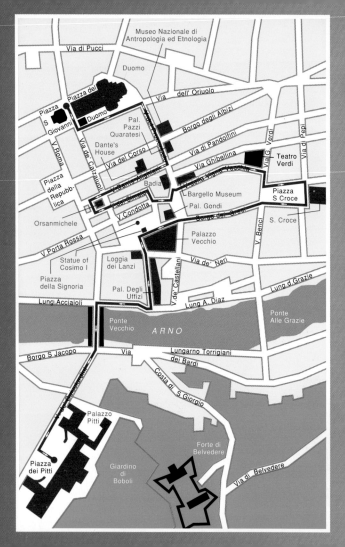

## Duomo - Palazzo Pitti

**2 hr 30 min** - *excluding visits to museums, galleries and churches.*

Together the Piazza del Duomo and the Piazza S Giovanni (collectively known as the Piazza del Duomo) form the religious heart of Florence, containing the Battistero (see **A-Z**), Duomo (see **CHURCHES 1**, **A-Z**) and Campanile. The oldest of these is the Baptistery, or Basilica di S Giovanni, which, historically and architecturally, is one of the most important buildings in the city. Walk round to the east door, Ghiberti's (see **A-Z**) 'Door of Paradise', facing the magnificent facade of the cathedral (where some of Florence's prominent soldiers, theologians and artists are commemorated). The famous bell-tower, the Campanile di Giotto, stands on its right.

Leave the piazza at the south-east corner and walk down the picturesque, narrow Via del Proconsolo, passing the Museo Nazionale di Antropologia ed Etnologia (see **MUSEUMS 2**) and the Palazzo Pazzi Quaratesi (on your left). Turn right into the Via Dante Alighieri and you soon come to Dante's (see **A-Z**) house on the corner of Via Santa Margherita, which now houses the Società delle Belle Arti and its small gallery (1000-1200, 1600-1930 Tues.-Sun.).

Keep going along the Via Dante Alighieri and the adjoining Via dei Tavolini, and then cross over the busy Via de' Calzaiuoli to Orsanmichele on the right (see **CHURCHES 2**, **A-Z**). Walk round the squarish building and admire the 15th and 16thC sculptures adorning the facades before taking the Via dei Cimatori at the south-east corner. Towards the end of the road you will see before you Florence's most splendid belfry: the tower of the Badia Fiorentina (see **CHURCHES 1**, **A-Z**). To reach the front of the Badia, turn right at the end of the road into the Via dei Magazzini, and then left into the Via Condotta, leading into the Piazza San Firenze. The Courthouse stands across the *piazza* on the right. Going left, back onto the Via del Proconsolo, you will see on the right the crenellated facade of the Bargello Museum (see **MUSEUMS 1**, **A-Z**), built during the decisive years of the struggle between the Guelphs and the Ghibellines (see **A-Z**). The Badia is opposite.

Walk along the Bargello's southern side on the Via della Vigna Vecchia. Carry on along the adjoining Via dei Lavatoi, and then turn right into the Via Giuseppe Verdi at the end of the street. Further along it, on your left, is the expanse of the Piazza S Croce (see **PIAZZE**, **A-Z**) containing the large Franciscan church of Santa Croce - known as the Florentine Pantheon because of the number of tombs of famous figures it contains (see **CHURCHES 2**, **A-Z**). Look around the many leather shops surrounding the square before taking the Borgo dei Greci at its western corner. Continue along the adjoining Via de' Gondi into the Piazza della Signoria (see **CAFÉS-BARS**, **PIAZZE**, **A-Z**), passing the Palazzo Vecchio (see **MUSEUMS 3**, **PALAZZI 1**, **A-Z**) on your left and the Palazzo Gondi (**PALAZZI 2**) on your right. The L-shaped Piazza della Signoria is the historic hub of the city's political life. The west side is dominated by the famous Palazzo Vecchio, in front of which is a copy of Michelangelo's *David* (see **A-Z**)

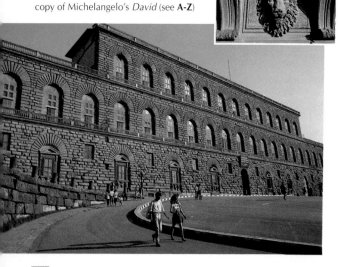

and the huge *Neptune Fountain* by Ammannati (1563-75). The latter is reckoned to be an artistic failure and has gained the nickname of *Il Biancone* (The Big White Thing). To the right of the palace is the graceful Loggia dei Lanzi, and to the left are the Tribunale di Mercanzia and the Palazzo Uguccioni (see **PALAZZI 2**). A large equestrian statue of Cosimo I stands in the centre of the *piazza*.

Leave the square by the Piazzale degli Uffizi between the Palazzo Vecchio and the Loggia dei Lanzi. This is the long narrow interior courtyard of the imposing Palazzo degli Uffizi which houses the impressive Galleria degli Uffizi (see **ART 1**, **UFFIZI**, **A-Z**). Just before the river turn right under the archway and cross the road to the arcades beside the river which run underneath the elevated covered walkway known as Vasari's (see **A-Z**) Corridoio, connecting the Palazzo Vecchio to the Palazzo Pitti. Follow it as it turns left onto the Ponte Vecchio (see **WALK 3**, **A-Z**) and walk across the bridge between the rows of little goldsmiths' and jewellers' shops .

Once on the other side of the Arno continue south along the Via de' Guicciardini to the Piazza dei Pitti which contains another of Florence's most famous palaces, the Palazzo Pitti, which became the grand-ducal residence of the Medicis (see **A-Z**) in the mid-16thC, and now houses museums and galleries (see **ART 1**, **MUSEUMS 3**, **PALAZZI 1**, **A-Z**). Explore the palace gardens, amongst the most magnificent in Italy, then cool off at the end of your walk with a superb, if rather costly, fresh *granita al limone* at the outdoor café (see **Giardino di Boboli**).

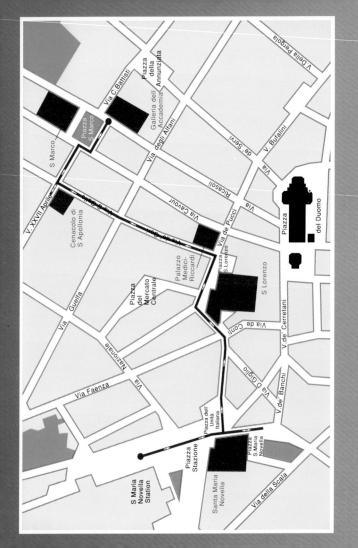

## Station - Accademia

*2 hr - excluding visits to museums, galleries and churches.*

From S Maria Novella Station walk over to the beautiful Romanesque-Gothic church and monastery of Santa Maria Novella (see **CHURCHES 2, A-Z**) on your right just south west of the Piazza dell'Unità Italiana. Note the *avelli* (niches) containing the tombs of noble Florentines in the facade of the church on your right, just before you come into the Piazza S. M. Novella - once the site of thrilling chariot races (see **PIAZZE**). The two marble obelisks were originally turning posts in the races. After visiting the church return to the Piazza dell'Unità Italiana and take the Via del Melarancio off the opposite side of the square, leading into the Piazza degli Aldobrandini.

The entrance to the splendid Medici Chapels stands across the *piazza* (see **Cappelle Medicee**). Walk round to the other side of the early Renaissance church of San Lorenzo (see **CHURCHES 2, A-Z**), designed by Brunelleschi, into the busy Piazza San Lorenzo, one of Florence's liveliest market squares (see **MARKETS, PIAZZE**). Across the square, on its north-eastern corner at the junction of the Via de' Ginori and the Via de' Gori, stands the Palazzo Medici-Riccardi (see **ART 2, PALAZZI 1, A-Z**). Follow the Via de' Ginori to the left of the palace and then the adjoining Via S Gallo, going in a northerly direction.

Turn left onto the Via XXVII Aprile and you soon come to the entrance of the Cenacolo di Sant'Apollonia (see **ART 2**). The long convent refectory contains Andrea del Castagno's most important frescoes including his powerful *Last Supper*. Turn right into the Via degli Arrazzieri leading to the Piazza San Marco, site of the Art School and the University. The Dominican church and convent of San Marco, occupying the north side of the square, contains the Fra Angelico Museum where you can see the luminous frescoes executed by the monk and his followers (see **CHURCHES 2, MUSEUMS 1, San Marco**). The impressive Galleria dell'Accademia (see **ART 1**), adjoining the Art School on the Via Ricasoli at the eastern end of the square, houses Michelangelo's famous *David* (see **A-Z**).

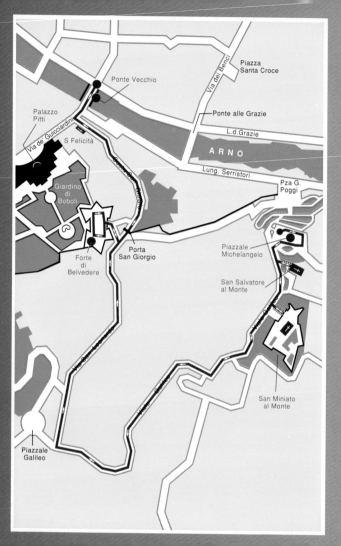

## Viale dei Colli

**3 hr.** Take Bus 13 from the Via del Proconsolo (behind Piazza del Duomo) to the Piazzale Michelangelo (see **A-Z**) and walk round this beautiful terrace to admire one of the city's most famous views. The bronze statues in the middle are reproductions of Michelangelo's *David* (see **A-Z**) and the four statues which decorate the Medici tombs in San Lorenzo (see **WALK 2**, **Cappelle Medicee**, **A-Z**).

Leaving the *piazzale,* cross Viale Galileo (also known as the Viale dei Colli - 'Avenue of the Hills') and climb the stairs behind La Loggia (see **CAFÉS, RESTAURANTS 1**) until you come to the 16thC Renaissance church of San Salvatore al Monte standing amidst the tall cypress trees.

Returning down the steps, turn left onto the Viale Galileo once again and climb the large white stairway on the left which leads to the Romanesque church of San Miniato al Monte (see **CHURCHES 2**, **A-Z**), whose magnificent green and white marble facade, with its splendid 13thC gold mosaic representing Christ on His throne blessing Mary and S Miniato, overlooks the city. The altar in the large 11thC crypt contains the bones of the martyr, S Miniato.

Return to the Viale Galileo. This tree-lined avenue offers breathtaking views of the city below as well as the surrounding countryside, dotted with villas and olive groves.

If you feel like a rest, sit down and have a cool drink in the garden of the Chalet Fontana bar on the right-hand side of the road about 1.5 km on. Then turn right into the enchanting Via San Leonardo, a quiet, typically narrow, country road lined with ancient garden walls and overhung by olive trees.

Continuing down the road, you will see the entrance to Forte di Belvedere on your left. Climb the stairs of this massive fortress and walk right round the grounds for more magnificent views. From here you can admire the Palazzo Pitti (see **PALAZZI 1**, **WALK 1**, **A-Z**) and the Boboli Gardens (see **WALK 1**, **Giardino di Boboli**). Return to the entrance, turn left through the ancient Porta San Giorgio and follow the picturesque Costa San Giorgio, a quaint, steep street. At the bottom of it stands the church of S Felicità (see **A-Z**) in the *piazza* of the same name.

Turn right into the Via de' Guicciardini leading to the Ponte Vecchio, the famous bridge lined with goldsmiths' and jewellers' shops (see **WALK 1**, **A-Z**).

**Accidents and Breakdowns:** In the event of an accident follow the usual procedure of exchanging names, addresses and insurance details. To contact the police or other emergency services, tel: 113 (see **Emergency Numbers**). If someone is injured and you are held responsible, insist on contacting your embassy or consulate as soon as possible (see **Consulates**).

In case of breakdowns, you should carry a red warning triangle (which can be hired from ACI offices - see **Driving**) with you at all times. This should be placed 50 m behind your vehicle before seeking help. Tel: 116 for ACI assistance. Other breakdown services include Radio Gen. Pantera, tel: (055) 372090 or 372087 (24 hr), and Soccorso Stradale (Garage CICLOP), tel: 287711. Emergency telephones line motorways at 1 km intervals - press the red button for medical assistance and the green button for breakdown assistance. Service and spare parts for Italian makes of car are easily obtainable; for other makes contact the relevant dealer in Florence.

**Accommodation:** The two main types of accommodation available in Florence are *pensioni* and hotels. *Pensioni* are generally cheaper, more informal and have fewer facilities than hotels in the same category, but the service is usually of an equally high standard. (More basic types of inn are known as *locande*.) The following figures indicate the price of a double room with bath in various categories of hotel:

5 star - L. 250,000-500,000; 3 star - L. 60,000-100,000; 1 star -
L. 35,000-40,000. Prices displayed in rooms (by law) are usually
exclusive of breakfast, but should include service charge and taxes;
check at reception so you know exactly what you are paying for, and
report any discrepencies in your final bill to the EPT (see **Tourist
Information**). It is necessary to book well in advance for both types of
accommodation during the high season or major events (see **Events**).
However, try the free booking service at the following ITA offices to
reserve a room on arrival: Stazione Centrale, tel: 282893 (0900-2030);
AGIP petrol station (on the A11 northbound motorway), tel: 440790;
Chianti East petrol station (A1 southbound), tel: 621349 (Apr.-Nov.);
Fortezza da Basso, tel: 471960. There is also a day hotel (*albergo
diurno*) at the station which rents rooms by the hour, where you can use
the shower or launderette facilities at a reasonable cost (0600-2000).
See **Camping, Youth Hostels**.

**Airports:** Galileo Galilei Airport near Pisa (83 km west of Florence) is
the closest international airport. There is a rail link (takes 1 hr) to
Florence's S Maria Novella Station, also known as Stazione Centrale or
Central Station (see **Railways**). Airport facilities include a restaurant,
bar, information desk, duty-free shop and car-hire representatives. Most
of the main airline companies operating from here have offices in
Florence. Ring (050) 28088 for flight information.
The Peretola Civic Airport at Via del Termine 11 (5 km north west of
Florence) handles internal Alitalia flights as well as flights to Nice,
Brussels, Munich and Paris. It also runs an Alitalia bus link to Central
Station. Ring (055) 317123 for flight information.

**Angelico, Fra (d.1455):** Guido di Pietro was born in Fiesole (see
**A-Z**). Little is known of his artistic training, but his deep piety led him
into the Dominican order and all his art was religious in nature. He was
one of the Renaissance's most celebrated and progressive artists and
many of his exquisitely-coloured works can be seen in the museum at
San Marco monastery, the cells of which are decorated with his famous
series of frescoes (see **CHURCHES 2, MUSEUMS 1, WALK 2, A-Z**). More of his
masterpieces can be seen in the Uffizi (see **WALK 1, A-Z**).

**Arezzo:** 85 km from Florence. Pop: 91,691. Train from Central Station (see **Railways**). Tourist information office (EPT): Piazza Risorgimento 116. The provincial capital had an illustrious past as an important Etruscan settlement, a prosperous Roman stronghold (you can still see the remains of the Roman amphitheatre), and a thriving independent city-state before it came under Florentine dominion in 1584. Now it is an agricultural and craft centre which hosts an annual international choral festival (Aug.), and a monthly Antiques Fair in the Piazza Grande (also the venue of a spectacular medieval joust every Sept.). See **EXCURSION 1**.

**Baby-sitters:** Enquire at hotel reception or ask your chambermaid. Costs L. 10,000-15,000 per hour plus transport home.

**Badia Fiorentina:** This former Benedictine abbey was founded in 978 by the mother of the Margrave of Tuscany. It was enlarged in 1285 by Arnolfo di Cambio and underwent further reconstruction in 1627 by Segaloni (who also designed the church's beautiful Baroque ceiling). The Romanesque-Gothic *campanile* dates from 1310-30. As you enter the church you will see Filippino Lippi's (see **A-Z**) masterpiece *The Apparition of the Virgin Mary to St Bernard* on the left. Among the tombs is that of Ugo, the founder's son, by Mino da Fiesole (in the left transept). The apse contains a magnificent fresco by Ferretti (1734), and scenes from *The Life of St Bernard* by Consalvo decorate the Chiostro degli Aranci to the right of the choir. See **CHURCHES 1**, **WALK 1**.

**Bargello:** This splendid medieval palace (1255) was built as the Palazzo del Popolo (the city's first town hall) before becoming the Palazzo del Podestà (seat of the city's magistrates). It has also served as a prison. Within these historic walls Dante (see **A-Z**) attended meetings of the Council of the Hundred, and Leonardo da Vinci (see **A-Z**) witnessed the hanging of Baroncelli, one of the Pazzi Conspirators (see **A-Z**). Its present name derives from the *bargello*, or chief of police, who moved his headquarters here in the 16thC. The National Sculpture Museum was established in the palace in 1859 and contains the largest collection of sculpture and bronzes in Italy. Among the chief exhibits are Michelangelo's famous marble bust of *Brutus* (1540), his unfinished *David* (1530), and Cellini's four bronze statues: *Danae and Perseus, Jove, Mercury* and *Minerva*. Visit the attractive courtyard. See **MUSEUMS 1, PALAZZI 1, WALK 1**.

**Baroque:** A style which prevailed in the art and architecture of the 17thC and is characterized by an uninhibited use of elaborate decoration.

**Battistero:** The Romanesque Baptistery of St John on the Piazza S Giovanni is a 11th-12thC octagonal building thought to occupy the site of a Roman palace dating from the 4th or 5thC. It is the city's oldest building and served as its cathedral for over a century. It is most notable for three magnificent sets of bronze doors. The earliest (1330), by Andrea Pisano, are the South Doors, decorated with panels depicting *The Life of St John the Baptist*, and the *Cardinal* and *Theological Virtues* (see **Pisano**). More famous still are the East Doors (facing the Duomo) which Michelangelo described as fit for the 'doors to Paradise'. They were designed by Lorenzo Ghiberti (see **A-Z**) who, in 1401, defeated Brunelleschi (see **A-Z**) in a competition held by one of the merchants' guilds to select the best artist to design these and the North Doors (both artists' plans can be seen in the Bargello Museum - see **A-Z**). Ghiberti's execution of the project was so successful he was made a city magistrate. The interior of the building is in stunning black and white marble and contains fine mosaics and tombs including that of Medici patron Baldasare Coscia (the antipope John XXIII). See **CITY SIGHTS, WALK 1**.

**Best Buys:** Florence is one of Italy's fashion centres and hosts two haute couture shows a year (see **Events**). Consequently, clothes sold here are usually of a high quality and very expensive. Locally produced leather garments and accessories of all kinds are much better value. Silk and handmade straw items (such as hats and baskets) are also local specialities. Florence has a long tradition of hand embroidery, and beautifully embroidered articles such as tablecloths and napkins make delightful presents. Antiques are also a major business, but some knowledge or guidance is advisable before making any expensive purchases (see **Events**). A good alternative is one of the excellent reproductions of famous statues or paintings. Bookbinding is another speciality as is the beautiful, but expensive, Florentine marbled paper (this can be bought by the sheet). Finally, there is a vast choice of reasonably-priced silverware and jewellery to suit both modern and traditional tastes. See **MARKETS, SHOPPING**.

**Biblioteca Laurenziana:** One of the most beautiful libraries in the world, situated next to the church of San Lorenzo (see **CHURCHES 2, WALK 2, A-Z**) at Piazza San Lorenzo 9 (0900-1300 Mon.-Sat.; free). Cardinal Guilio de' Medici (later Pope Clement VII) commissioned

Michelangelo (see **A-Z**) to design it as a repository for the valuable Medici collections of books, manuscripts and documents which he had inherited from Cosimo the Elder and Lorenzo the Magnificent. Michelangelo oversaw the building of the dramatic staircase, but the rest of his design, including the ornate vestibule, was completed by Vasari (see **A-Z**) and Ammannati to his specifications. Among its numerous treasures are a 5thC Virgil codex and a MS of Horace annotated by Petrarch.

**Bicycle and Motorbike Hire:** Florence and its surrounding countryside are easily accessible by bicycle. These can be hired from Ciao & Basta, Via L. Alamanni (corner of the Piazza Stazione), tel: 263985 (spring/summer) and the bus/car park at Fortezza da Basso, tel: 499319 (summer only). Cost: L. 10,000 per day; L. 40,000 per week; L. 120,000 per month.

To hire a motorbike or scooter you must be over 18 and hold a valid licence. You can hire both types of vehicle from Motorrent, Via San Zanobi 9r, tel: 490113; motorbikes only from Program Borgognissanti

96, tel: 282916; and motorbikes or mopeds from Sabra Via degli Artisti 8, tel: 576256. A scooter from Motorrent costs L. 55,000 per day (includes 100 km) or L. 300,000 per week (includes 700 km).

**Boccaccio, Giovanni (1313-75):** A famous Florentine writer and humanist whose most famous work is *The Decameron*, a collection of 100 tales narrated by a group of young nobles undergoing self-exile in the Florentine countryside to escape from the plague-ridden city. Shakespeare, Chaucer and Keats are just a few of the poets who have drawn inspiration from the work of 'the father of the novel'. He lived and died in the medieval town of Certaldo Alto, where you can visit his house and tomb as well as a museum and library dedicated to his work and influence (see **EXCURSION 3**).

**Botticelli, Sandro (1444-1510):** This famous pupil of Fra Filippo Lippi (see **A-Z**) began his career as a religious painter and, like many of the progressive painters of his time, turned to Classical myths and allegories for subject matter. As a convert of the eloquent Savonarola (see **A-Z**), he returned to Christian art with almost fanatical fervour. He ranks among the great painters of women and his rather wan ideal of feminine beauty was much admired by the Pre-Raphaelites. His *Birth of Venus*, *Primavera* and *Madonna of the Magnificat* all hang in the Uffizi. See **UFFIZI 1**.

**Brunelleschi, Filippo (1377-1446):** The creator of the Renaissance style of architecture was originally trained as a goldsmith before becoming a sculptor. He then abandoned sculpture and turned exclusively to architecture when his designs for the Baptistery doors were rejected in favour of Ghiberti's (see **Battistero**). One of his greatest achievements was solving the technical difficulties inherent in placing the cupola on the octagonal base of the Duomo (see **CHURCHES 1**, **WALK 1**, **A-Z**). He also designed the lovely churches of Santo Spirito (see **CHURCHES 1**, **A-Z**) and San Lorenzo (see **CHURCHES 2**, **WALK 2**, **A-Z**), and the delightful Cappella dei Pazzi (see **A-Z**). His studies of Classical proportions led to him becoming known as the inventor of mechanical perspective.

**Budget:**

| | | |
|---|---|---|
| Bread | L.3000 per kilo. |
| Butter | L.3300 per 250 g. |
| Eggs | L.3000 per doz. |
| Steak | L.9000-10,000 per kilo. |
| Fruit juice | L.4000 per litre. |
| Wine | from L.3000 per bottle. |
| Hotel Breakfast | L.8000-12,000 |
| Dish of the Day | L.8000-10,000 |
| Beer | L.3000 per glass. |
| House wine | from L.3500 per bottle. |
| Brandy | from L.4000 per glass. |

See **Accommodation**.

**Buses:** The ATAF bus company operates within Florence. Information, tickets and a free map can be obtained from their office at Piazza del Duomo 57r, tel: 212301. Tickets are also sold in bars (displaying ATAF stickers in the window) and tobacconists, and there are automatic ticket machines at some of the main stops in the centre. They cost L. 600 for a single trip and L. 700 for journeys of up to 70 minutes. Books of eight tickets and passes are also available. Enter buses at the rear and pass your ticket through the machine by the door. Several companies operate reasonably-priced reliable services from Florence to the rest of Tuscany and destinations throughout Italy. Contact the EPT office for details (see **Tourist Information**).

**Cameras and Photography:** Most well-known makes of film and other photographic equipment are widely available in Florence, but films do tend to be expensive so bring a stock with you. There are no restrictions on taking photos in the national museums, but it is prohibited in municipal museums without prior authorization.

**Camping:** There are two official camp sites in Florence itself. The cost of a night at the one at Viale Michelangelo 80 is L. 4400 per adult, L. 3500 per child, L. 4000 per tent or car and L. 5000 per caravan. The other, Camerata, is situated in the park of the Youth Hostel (see **A-Z**) and costs L. 3700 per adult, L. 6200 for a four-person tent, L. 4350 for a

two-person tent and L. 8000 per caravan.
There are another three sites outside the city:
Fiesole - Camping Panoramico, Via Peramondo 1, tel: 599069.
Bottai (near Galluzzo) - Camping Internazionale Firenze, Via Cristofare
2, tel: 2034704.
Calenzano (near motorway exit for Firenze Nord) - Via Vittorio
Emanuele II, tel: 882391.
For further information about their facilities contact Centro
Internazionale Prenotazioni Campeggio, CP 23-50041 Calenzano,
Firenze, or the EPT office (see **Tourist Information**). Camping outside
official sites in isolated areas is strongly discouraged by the police
because of the 'Mostro di Firenze', a maniac who has been known to
kill young couples.

**Cappelle Medicee:** The Medici Chapels in the church of San
Lorenzo (see **CHURCHES 2, A-Z**) were commissioned by Cosimo I to
house the family tombs. The floor plan of the 16th-17thC Cappella dei
Principi (Chapel of the Princes) is based on that of the Battistero (see
**WALK 2, A-Z**). The extravagant interior took several centuries to com-
plete. It contains two large bronze portraits of Cosimo II and
Ferdinando I by Tacca.
The Sagrestia Nuova was Michelangelo's first architectural creation,
although he never finished it. On the left-hand side is the tomb of
Lorenzo de' Medici (grandson of Lorenzo the Magnificent), decorated
with allegorical figures of *Evening* and *Dawn*. This is complemented on
the right-hand side by the figures of *Day* and *Night* on the tomb of
Guiliano de' Medici. See **WALK 2, Medicis**.

**Cappella dei Pazzi:** This beautifully-proportioned chapel (c.1430)
beside the church of Santa Croce (see **CHURCHES 2, WALK 1, A-Z**) bears
all the hallmarks of Brunelleschi's (see **A-Z**) style of architecture. He
designed it for the tombs of the Pazzi family, rivals of the Medicis (see
**A-Z**) and perpetrators of the infamous Pazzi Conspiracy (see **A-Z**). Their
downfall occurred before the chapel was completed and no members
of the family are buried here. The 12 terracotta roundels of the apostles
are by Luca della Robbia.

**Car Hire:** Although a car is not of much use in Florence itself (because of traffic restrictions, parking difficulties, etc), you may want to hire one to tour the beautiful Tuscan countryside (see **EXCURSIONS**). To do so you must have held a licence for at least one year and be over 21 years of age.

Most of the major international car-hire companies have offices in town, at the airport and at the station (you can arrange to collect a car on your arrival - ask for a discount when booking in advance). The main Avis office is at Borgognissanti 128r (tel: 213629) and Hertz is at Via M. Finiguerra 33 (tel: 282260). Unless you are paying by credit card you will have to leave a deposit. Local companies are usually 20-25% cheaper and can offer foreigners special weekend rates and unlimited mileage for weekly hire (third-party insurance is always included). A list of these can be obtained at your hotel or the EPT (see **Tourist Information**). The cost of a Fiat Panda is L. 35,000 per day, plus L. 550 per km. See **Driving, Parking**.

**Cascine:** This large public park, covering three kilometres of land along the north bank of the Arno, was originally the site of dairy farms owned by the Medicis (see **A-Z**). In the 17thC it became a grand-ducal hunting ground, and was not opened to the public until the early 19thC. Shelley composed *Ode to the West Wind* here in 1819. There are numerous restaurants, cafés, sports facilites, and a weekly market (see **MARKETS**, **Sports**). Visit the Monumento dell'Indiano at the far end, erected in memory of the Maharajah of Kolhapur who died in Florence in 1870. Avoid wandering around the park alone at night.

**Castagno, Andrea del (c.1421-57):** This leading Florentine painter is best known for his frescoes, the most important of which are *The Last Supper*, and the *Crucifixion, Deposition* and *Resurrection* in the refectory of Sant'Apollonia (see **ART 2**), now the Castagno Museum.

**Cellini, Benvenuto (1500-71):** The celebrated Florentine gold-smith and sculptor worked for popes Clement VII and Paul III in Rome, as well as the French court of Francis I (where he gained experience in bronze-casting). On his return to Florence he executed the bronze

*Perseus*, commissioned by Cosimo I, which stands inside the Loggia dei Lanzi in the Piazza della Signoria (see **PIAZZE**, **A-Z**). His *Autobiography*, which describes the casting of the statue, is interesting for what it reveals about the artistic and intellectual life of the time and about the artist's own bizarre personality.

**Chemists:** Most chemists keep normal opening hours (see **Opening Times**), but they also operate a rota system so that at least one shop is open outside normal hours. Details are displayed in the window of every chemist under *ore di turno*. The same list is published in the local newspaper *La Nazione*, or you can phone 192. The following are 24-hr chemists: Communale No. 13, Stazione S M. Novella (tel: 263435); Molteni, Via Calzaiuoli 7r (tel: 263490); Taverna, Piazza del Duomo 20r (tel: 284013).

**Cimabue (1240-1302):** Described by Vasari (see **A-Z**) in his *Lives* as Giotto's (see **A-Z**) teacher. Although only the mosaic in Pisa Cathedral (see **EXCURSION 2**) is known to have been his work, *The Crucifixion* in the museum at Santa Croce (see **MUSEUMS 2**) and the S

Trinità *Madonna* in the Uffizi (see **UFFIZI 2**) are attributed to him.

**Climate:** The most pleasant times of the year to visit Florence are early summer and autumn. The weather in spring can be very changeable and it can get quite cold in winter and oppressively hot and sticky in the height of summer. Rain is most frequent during the months of November, January and April.

**Complaints:** If you have been overcharged ask to see the owner or manager of the premises. If you are still not satisfied, then you can report the establishment to the EPT (see **Tourist Information**) or the police (see **A-Z**), but you will find that just threatening this course of action is usually sufficient.

**Consulates:**
UK          Lungarno Corsini 2, tel: 284133.
USA        Lungarno Amerigo Vespucci 38, tel: 298276.

**Conversion Charts:**

**TEMPERATURE**

°C   −30 −25 −20 −15 −10 −5   0   5   10  15  20  25  30  35  40  45
°F        −20 −10   0   10  20  30  40  50  60  70  80  90  100 110

**DISTANCE**

kms   0   1   2   3   4   5   6       8       10      12      14      16
miles 0  ½   1  1½   2       3       4       5   6   7   8   9   10

**WEIGHT**

grams   0   100  200  300  400  500  600  700  800  900   1 kg
ounces  0      4      8      12    1 lb   20    24    28    2 lb

**Crime and Theft:** Although Florence is no worse than any other large city in this respect, you should keep all valuables and large amounts of cash in the hotel safe. Carry your wallet in a secure pocket, and handbags under the arm rather than over the shoulder. Never leave baggage unattended or visible in a motor vehicle. Keep a separate list of the numbers of your traveller's cheques along with a note of your passport number. If the former are stolen go to the nearest American Express office immediately or, if they are not American Express cheques, notify the office where they were issued. Report the loss of a passport to the police and your consulate (see **A-Z**). Carry car documents with you to prove ownership in case of theft. Keep a copy of police reports for insurance claims.

**Currency:** The lira is the national monetary unit of Italy (abbreviated as L.; plural lire). Coins in circulation are worth 10, 20, 50, 100, 200 and 500 lire. Notes are in denominations of 1000, 2000, 5000, 10,000, 50,000 and 100,000 lire. Due to the scarcity of anything smaller than a L. 50 coin, you may be given sweets, matches or *gettoni* (telephone tokens) in place of small change.

**Customs:**

| Duty Paid Into: | Cigarettes | *or* Cigars | *or* Tobacco | Spirits | Wine |
|---|---|---|---|---|---|
| E.E.C. | 300 | 75 | 400 g | 1.5 *l* | 5 *l* |
| U.K. | 300 | 75 | 400 g | 1.5 *l* | 5 *l* |

**Dante Alighieri (1265-1321):** Italy's greatest poet was a native of Florence, but was exiled in 1302 for his political involvements. Thereafter he led a wandering existence, finally dying in Ravenna where he found refuge in his last years. His greatest work was the

*Divina Commedia* (*Divine Comedy*), comprising the *Inferno* (*Hell*), the *Purgatorio* (*Purgatory*) and the *Paradiso* (*Heaven*).

**David:** Michelangelo's famous sculpture (1501-04) originally stood in front of the Palazzo Vecchio (see **PALAZZI 1**, **A-Z**) on the Piazza della Signoria (see **PIAZZE**, **WALK 1**, **A-Z**), as a symbol of Florence's civic pride and independence. The huge, perfectly-proportioned figure of the powerful yet slender youth is sculpted out of a block of white Carrara marble. It was moved to the Accademia (see **ART 1**) in 1873, where it is still housed, and a copy was put in its place. Another copy stands on the Piazzale Michelangelo (see **WALK 3**, **A-Z**). See **Michelangelo**.

**Disabled:** Florence is not an easy city to negotiate if you are in a wheelchair. Most of the buildings are old and ill-equipped for the disabled, although a few have lifts. Contact the EPT (see **Tourist Information**) for a list of places catering for particular disabilities, and mention any special needs when making a hotel reservation.

**Donatello (1386-1466):** Donato di Niccolò Betto Bardi was one of the greatest and most original of Italy's Renaissance sculptors. He trained in the workshop of Florence's Duomo (see **CHURCHES 1**, **A-Z**) and executed many works for it and other church buildings throughout the city, including the Battistero (see **CITY SIGHTS**, **A-Z**), the Campanile (see **CITY SIGHTS**), Orsanmichele (see **CHURCHES 2**, **A-Z**), S Lorenzo (see **CHURCHES 2**, **A-Z**) and S Croce (see **CHURCHES 2**, **A-Z**). His famous *St George* and the magnificent bronze *David* are in the Bargello (see

MUSEUMS 1, **A-Z**). Many more of his powerfully expressive works can be seen in the Museo dell'Opera del Duomo (see **MUSEUMS 1**).

**Drinks:** Tuscany's most famous speciality is Chianti wine, a light red wine of which there are several different varieties, the best being Chianti Classico. You can try any of the region's wines at the following *cantine*: Cantina Ricasoli, Via delle Mantellate 9r; Cantina Antinori, Piazza Antinori 3; Cantina degli Albizi, Borgo Albizi 72. In a restaurant the cheapest wine you can order is house wine (*vino della casa*). Other popular alcoholic drinks include *vin santo* (a sweet amber-coloured liqueur), *grappa* (a strong colourless spirit made from grape skins) and *birra* (lager).

Non-alcoholic drinks include *tamarindo* (made from tamarind fruit and very refreshing) and *spremuta* (freshly-squeezed fruit juice). The usual range of fizzy drinks is also widely available.

Tap water is drinkable, but tastes strongly of chlorine - still or sparkling bottled water is preferable. If you ask for coffee (*un caffè*) you will be served an espresso, a small cup of strong black coffee. If you want a lit-tle milk in it, order it *macchiato*. For plain white coffee ask for a *caffel-latte*. A cappuccino is an espresso with frothy milk and a sprinkling of chocolate. Tea is not widely drunk in Italy, but most places offer it to tourists.

**Driving:** Third-party insurance is obligatory when driving in Italy. Make sure you have your driving licence and car registration papers and that you are displaying a national identity sticker. You must also carry a red warning triangle in case of breakdowns (see **Accidents and Breakdowns**). The wearing of seat belts is compulsory. Petrol coupons (giving discounts on petrol) and motorway vouchers (for use at motor-way tolls) are available for foreign motorists bringing their cars into the country (but not if you hire a car in Italy). These are available from automobile associations in your own country or Automobile Club Italiano (ACI) branches at border crossings (not within Italy). The ACI offers reciprocal membership to members of affiliated foreign auto-mobile associations and will come to your aid if you have a break-down.

The speed limit is 130 kph on motorways from Mon.-Fri. and 110 kph on Sat. and Sun.; 90 kph on main roads; and 50 kph in built-up areas. Fines for speeding are hefty and have to be paid on the spot (ask for a receipt). Drive on the right-hand side of the road and remember that traffic from the right has priority unless otherwise indicated. Petrol stations usually close between 1200-1500 and after 1900. The police have a list of those which stay open all night. Traffic in the centre of Florence is severely restricted and it is best to leave your car at an official car park outside the city (see **Parking**). See **Car Hire**.

**Drugs:** All drugs are illegal and there are severe penalties for offenders. Contact your embassy or consulate (see **A-Z**) if you are arrested for a drugs-related offence.

**Duomo:** In 1294 Arnolfo di Cambio (1245-c.1302) was commissioned to build the cathedral of S Maria del Fiore on the site of the church which was the old cathedral. The new structure was intended to reflect the city's increasing importance as a trading and finance centre, and to serve its growing population. Construction took over a century and was carried on by a number of architects, including Talenti. It was not until the end of the 19thC that the facade was finally completed. Brunelleschi overcame enormous technical difficulties in surmounting the chancel with the colossal dome (1420-34), and it is well worth climbing the 436 steps up to the lantern (added in 1461, after his death) for a view of the city and a closer look at his work (see **Brunelleschi**). The cruciform interior, with its three tribunes each surrounded by five chapels, has a Gothic starkness contrasting sharply with the colourful exterior. A fresco of *The Last Judgement* by Vasari (see **A-Z**) and Zuccari covers the inside of the dome, and beneath it is the fine marble balustrade which surrounds the chancel. The lunettes over the entrances to the sacristies are decorated with terracotta reliefs of the *Ascension* and *Resurrection* by della Robbia. It was in the Sagrestia delle Messe, with its bronze doors by Lucca, that Lorenzo the Magnificent escaped being murdered by the Pazzi Conspirators (see **A-Z**). Steps from the south aisle lead down to the crypt of S Reparata and the excavations of earlier churches. See **CHURCHES 1, WALK 1**.

**Eating Out:** Florence has many restaurants, most offering excellent food and service, but to be sure of getting value for money and an authentic atmosphere try the trattorias - informal, often family-run businesses, serving traditional regional dishes. The bill usually includes a service and cover charge (10-20%). It is also customary to leave a tip (see **Tipping**). If you are looking for Italian fast food try a *tavola calda* - a counter serving hot meals (sometimes a cheaper restaurant serving hot meals and not particularly fast). See RESTAURANTS, **Food**.

**Electricity:** 220 volts. Small two-pin plugs are used and adaptors are available in Italy and the UK.

### Emergency Numbers:

| | |
|---|---|
| Police | 113. |
| Carabinieri | 112. |
| Traffic Police | 352141. |
| Ambulance | 113 or 212222. |
| Fire | 113 or 115. |
| Night Doctor | 4976. |
| Emergency Dentist | 575411 (Tourist Medical Service). |
| Cardiographic Unit | 214444. |
| ACI Road Service | 116 (see **Driving**). |

**Events:**

*Mar.* - Spring Fashion Shows in the Palazzo Pitti (see **PALAZZI 1, A-Z**); *25* - Festa dell'Annunziata with fair in the Piazza della SS Annunziata (see **PIAZZE, A-Z**).

*Easter* - Scoppio del carro, a float loaded with fireworks is drawn by white bulls to the Duomo (see **CHURCHES 1, A-Z**).

*Ascension* - Festa del grillo, sale of caged crickets in the Cascine Park.

*Spring* - Antique auctions at Sotheby Parke Bernet, Via Gino Capponi and Casa d'Aste Pitti, Via Maggio.

*Apr.-May* - Mostra dell'artigianato, craft show at the Fortezza da Basso (see **A-Z**).

*Apr.-June* - Mostra di piante fiori, flower show at the Piazza della Signoria (see **PIAZZE, WALK 1, A-Z**) and the Uffizi (see **UFFIZI, WALK 1, A-Z**).

*Mid May-July* - Maggio musicale, festival of orchestral concerts, ballets and operas (see **Music**).

*24 June* - Festa di S Giovanni, St John's Day (Florence's patron saint) when the general festivities include the Giuoco del calcio (a football game played in medieval costume) on the Piazza S Croce (see **PIAZZE, WALK 1, A-Z**) and evening fireworks on the Piazzale Michelangelo (see **WALK 3, A-Z**).

*June-Aug.* - Estate Fiesolana, a festival of music, drama and film.

*7 Sept.* - Festa delle rificolone, a riverside procession with lanterns.

*Autumn* - Mostra dell'antiquariato, antiques fair in the Palazzo Strozzi (see **PALAZZI 1, A-Z**), and antique auctions (see *Mar.* above).

*Oct.* - Autumn fashion shows at the Palazzo Pitti (see *Spring* above). Tickets for various events are sold at Universalturismo, Via degli Speziali 5r and Box Office, Via della Pergola 10/a r. See **Public Holidays**.

**Fiesole:** 8 km north east of Florence. Pop: 14,800. Bus 7 from San Marco. Tourist office: Piazza Mino da Fiesole 45, tel: 598720.
The ancient town of Fiesole stands on the summit of a wooded hill overlooking Florence and the Arno, and affords magnificent views of the countryside. Founded around the 7thC BC, it was one of the most important cities of Etruria. However, its Etruscan remains are poor in

comparison to the Roman excavations, which are of the utmost interest. The city flourished under the Lombardian regime, but was ravaged by the Florentines in 1125. Now it is an attractive residential district with some fine villas. It is highly recommended as a worthwhile destination for a short half-day excursion.

**Food:** Florentine cuisine is simple yet refined, mainly consisting of tasty soups, grilled, roasted and stewed meats, seasonal fruits and vegetables, and local cheeses. Some of the more popular dishes include:
*prosciutto crudo con fichi* - raw ham with figs.
*crostini di fegatini* - croutons with chicken liver pâté.
*bistecca alla fiorentina* - famous thick sirloin steak.
*trippa alla fiorentina* - tripe with ham, tomatoes and parmesan cheese.
*fagioli all'uccelletto* - butter beans in a tomato, onion and sage sauce.
*baccalà alla fiorentina* - cod stew.
*zuccotto* - chilled chocolate sponge soaked in liqueur.
*gelato* - Italy's famous ice-cream, a must.
See **RESTAURANTS**, **Eating Out**.

**Forte di Belvedere:** See **WALK 3**.

**Fortezza da Basso:** This huge fortress, standing on the Viale Filippo Strozzi north east of the station, was built by Alessandro de' Medici partly to intimidate the citizens of Florence and his rivals and partly as

a place of refuge. Despite his efforts he was killed here by his cousin Lorenzino. The interior is open for exhibitions only.

**Galileo Galilei (1564-1642):** The Italian physicist, astronomer and philosopher was born in Pisa (see **EXCURSION 2**) of a Florentine family and moved to Florence in 1610 to take up the position of court mathematician. He invented the telescope and detected the moons of Jupiter, sunspots, mountains on the moon and many stars (see **MUSEUMS 2**). His support of the Copernican theory brought him into conflict with the Pope and he was accused of heresy by the Inquisition and was imprisoned for his scientific beliefs.

**Galleria degli Uffizi:** See **UFFIZI**, Uffizi.

**Ghiberti, Lorenzo (1378-1455):** The famous Renaissance sculptor, goldsmith, architect, painter and writer spent 21 years sculpting the bronze doors of the Battistero (see **WALK 1**, **A-Z**). He was one of the major artists involved in the transition from Gothic to Renaissance styles in art and his workshop trained many of the leading Renaissance figures.

**Ghirlandaio, Domenico (1449-94):** The religious frescoes produced by this painter record the faces, customs and manners of his contemporaries. This is most true of his cycle depicting *The Life of St John the Baptist* in the church of Santa Maria Novella (see **CHURCHES 2**, **A-Z**), which documents an entire era of social history. See **ART 2**.

**Giardino di Boboli:** Niccolò Pericoli (Tribolo) designed and began the landscaping of the gardens on the site of the quarry which provided the stone for the Palazzo Pitti. He died before completing his ambitious plans for the site and a series of architects (including Tasso, Ammannati, Buontalenti, and Giulio and Alfonso Parigi) carried his work on into the 17thC. In the 18thC the gardens were opened to the public who, for the first time, could enjoy its numerous delights, such as Buontalenti's mythical Grotto (decorated with frescoes and statues), Bandinelli's rustic Grotticina, Ammannatti's Roman Amphitheatre,

Lorenzi's Neptune Fountain, and the beautiful Viottolone (Avenue of Cypresses) with its water garden and wonderful views. Higher up on the slope is the Giardino del Cavaliere containing Tacca's famous fountain, decorated with statues of apes, and the Museo delle Porcellane (see **MUSEUMS 3**). See **Palazzo Pitti**.

**Giotto di Bondone (c.1267-1337):** The revolutionary Florentine painter and architect who broke with the static symbolism of medieval painting and brought life and realism into art; in this he was the founder of Renaissance painting. A pupil of Cimabue's (see **A-Z**), his talent soon exceeded his teacher's and he was put on the commune's payroll.

He painted four chapels in Santa Croce (see **CHURCHES 2**, **WALK 1**, **A-Z**), although only the frescoes in the Bardi and Peruzzi Chapels survive. You can also see his *Ognissanti Madonna* in the Uffizi (see **UFFIZI 1**). As city architect, he designed the Campanile (see **WALK 1**) for the Duomo (see **CHURCHES 1**, **A-Z**).

**Gothic:** A style of European architecture prevalent in the 12th-16thC, characterized by narrow pillars, pointed arches and high vaults.

**Guelphs and Ghibellines:** These two political factions originated in 1215 after the murder of Buondemonte de' Buondelmonti, a member of one of the great Florentine families. The Guelphs were in favour of the supremacy of the papacy, whereas the Ghibellines supported the Emperor. The two parties were in continual conflict during the 13thC, each struggling for government of the city, and there were many battles between them. The Guelphs later split into two rival factions: the Bianchi (Whites) and the Neri (Blacks). Dante (see **A-Z**) supported the Whites and was sent into permanent exile for his allegiance.

**Guides:** The official guide agency is Guide Turistiche at Viale Gramsci 9/a, tel: 2478188. Agriturist at Piazza S Firenze 3 (tel: 287838) organizes tours of Florence and its surrounding farms (Sept.-Oct.) and villas (April-June), as well as coach trips to Pisa (see **EXCURSION 2**), Siena (see **EXCURSION 1, A-Z**) and San Gimignano (see **EXCURSION 3**).

**Hairdressers:** There are numerous salons around the city, many of which are extremely stylish and expensive. You should expect to pay, on average, L. 20,000-25,000 for a shampoo and set or blow-dry, and L. 35,000-40,000 for a cut and set or blow-dry.
Women's hairdressers: Dante, Lungarno Corsini 36r (tel: 294893); Mario, Via Vigna Nuova, 22r (tel: 294813); Sergio & Mario, Piazza Strozzi (tel: 287354). Men's hairdressers: Giampaolo, Via Il Prato 70 (tel: 284643); Stefano, Piazza Frescobaldi 3 (tel: 287636).

**Health:** Before leaving the UK you should obtain form E 111 from the Department of Social Security which entitles you to free medical treatment in Italy. Present it to any (State) doctor you consult, who will arrange for you to be exempted from payment. You should also take out a private health insurance policy to cover the cost of repatriation in case of serious illness. The following are general hospitals:
Ospedale di Santa Maria Nuova, Piazza di S M. Nuova 1, tel: 27581.
Careggi, Viale Morgagni 85, tel: 43991; Nouvo Ospedale S Giovanni di Dio, Torre Galli, Via Torre Galli 3, tel: 27661; Istituto Ortopedico Toscano (IOT), Viale Michelangelo 41, tel: 27691.
The Tourist Medical Service also operates a 24-hr service manned by

English and French-speaking doctors at Via L. Il Magnifico (tel: 575411); and there is a children's hospital, the Anna Meyer Hospital, at Via L Giordano 13 (tel: 43991). See **Emergency Numbers, Insurance**.

**Insurance:** You should take out travel insurance covering you against theft and loss of property and money, as well as medical expenses, for the duration of your stay. Your travel agent should be able to recommend a suitable policy. See also **Crime and Theft**, **Driving**, **Health**.

**Laundries:** Ask at your hotel for the nearest launderette or go to the one at the day hotel at the station (see **Accommodation**). Prices are the same whether you have a service wash or do it yourself.

**Leonardo da Vinci (1452-1519):** Son of a Florentine lawyer, Leonardo was an artist, man of science and philosopher who was much admired in his home city. Among his many scientific interests were anatomy (he performed dissections) and the laws governing flight. He was less prolific as an artist, but two of his works, *The Adoration of the Magi* and *The Annunciation*, can be seen in the Uffizi (see **UFFIZI 2**). His most famous works are the *Mona Lisa*, which is in the Louvre in Paris, and *The Last Supper*, which is in Milan. See **EXCURSION 4**.

**Lippi, Filippino (c.1457-1504):** The son of Fra Filippo Lippi (see below) and a gifted pupil of Botticelli (see **A-Z**). His most important works include the completion of Masaccio's and Masolino's frescoes in the Brancacci Chapel (see **ART 2**) of Santa Maria del Carmine (see **CHURCHES 1, A-Z**), *The Vision of St Bernard* in the Badia Fiorentina (**CHURCHES 1, WALK 1, A-Z**) and *The Lives of SS Philip and John* in the Strozzi Chapel of Santa Maria Novella (see **CHURCHES 2, WALK 2, A-Z**).

**Lippi, Fra Filippo (c.1406-69):** Although the painter forsook his vows and married the ex-nun who modelled for him and bore his son Filippino (see above), he continued to sign himself 'Frater Philippus' and produce remarkably distinctive religious works which clearly reflect Masaccio's influence. His favourite subject matter was the *Madonna and Child*, the best examples of which can be seen in the

Uffizi (see **UFFIZI 1, WALK 1, A-Z**) and the Pitti (see **ART 1, PALAZZI 1, WALK 1, Palazzo Pitti**).

**Lost Property:** Can be claimed at the Lost Property Office, Via Circondaria 19, tel: 367943 (0900-1200 Mon.-Sat.). Also contact your consulate (see **A-Z**) for lost papers or documents as these are automatically passed on to them.

Anything lost on trains can be retrieved from the Lost Property Office which is situated at the far end of Platforms 1 and 2 in Santa Maria Novella Station (see **Railways**). For anything lost in taxis contact the relevant taxi office before trying the office on Via Circondaria (see above). If you do not manage to recover your lost property, report it to the police and get a copy of their report. This will have to be submitted for your insurance claim. See **Insurance**.

**Machiavelli, Niccolò (1469-1527):** The Florentine statesman and political theorist held office in the Medici administration for many years. He is best known for writing *The Prince*, a treatise on statecraft which he dedicated to Lorenzo the Magnificent.

**Masaccio (1401-c.1428):** Tommaso di Ser Giovanni di Mone was Florence's most influential artist after Giotto (see **A-Z**), and the first to really master the use of perspective. His frescoes (done in collaboration with Masolino) in the Brancacci Chapel (see **ART 2**) in S Maria del Carmine (see **CHURCHES 1, A-Z**), especially *The Tribute Money*, and his *Trinity* in the church of S. M. Novella (see **CHURCHES 2, WALK 2, A-Z**) are probably the most innovative works of the period and were very influential, being studied by every major artist of the Renaissance including Michelangelo. See **A-Z**.

**Medicis:** The great Florentine family of merchants and bankers held power in the city from 1464 until the 18thC. Among the most famous members of the dynasty, which provided Italy and western Europe with popes, patrons and rulers, were Cosimo the Elder (1389-1464), who virtually ruled Florence for over 30 years; his grandson Lorenzo the Magnificent (1449-92), who was a great patron of the arts and brilliant politician (Florence became the intellectual and artistic capital of Europe under his leadership); and Lorenzo II de' Medici (1492-1519), father of Catherine de' Medici who became a Queen of France (as did Maria, Cosimo I's granddaughter). Popes Leon X (1471-1521) and Clement VII (1478-1534) also belonged to this illustrious family.

**Mercato Sant'Ambrogio:** Like the Mercato Centrale (see **MARKETS**), this typical old food market, on the Piazza L. Ghiberti (north west of Santa Croce), is also located in a 19thC cast-iron building. Besides fresh produce you will also see flowers, clothing, footware and second-hand goods for sale here every day of the week apart from Sundays and holidays (0700-1330).

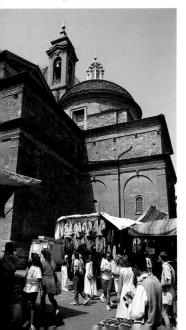

**Michelangelo (1475-1564):** Michelangelo Buonarroti is most famous as the painter of the Cistine Chapel in St Peter's, Rome, although he was also an architect, draughtsman and poet. He spent his life in Florence and Rome working alternately under the patronage of the Medicis and Pope Julius II, but it was in Rome that he really established his artistic reputation before returning to Florence in triumph in 1501. You can see his *Bacchus* in the Bargello (see **MUSEUMS 1, WALK 1, A-Z**) and his monumental *David* (see **A-Z**) in the Accademia (see **ART 2**). The Medici Chapels (see **CITY SIGHTS, WALK 2, Cappelle Medicee**) in San Lorenzo (see **CHURCHES 2, A-Z**) are among his other major undertakings. See **Museo Michelangelo**.

**Money:** Foreign currency and traveller's cheques can be changed in banks and bureaux de change on the production of a passport. Major credit cards are widely accepted and many shops and hotels also accept payment by traveller's cheques or in foreign currency, but often charge a high commission (check the rate they offer first). Major banks include the American Service Bank, Via della Vigna Nuova 2r, tel: 218141 (0830-2030 Mon.-Sat.); Banca d'Italia, Via dell'Oriuolo 37-9, tel: 1234001; and Citibank Italia, Viale del Poggio Imperiale, tel: 2280341. See **Crime and Theft**, **Currency, Opening Times**.

**Museo Bardini:** The eccentric Stefano Bardini (he never allowed himself to be photographed) was one of the most famous collectors of all time. He donated his palace and entire collection to the city of Florence in 1923 when he was 86. See MUSEUMS 2.

**Museo dell'Opera del Duomo:** Housed in the administrative offices of the cathedral, this museum contains some of Florence's most important pieces of Renaissance sculpture, the majority of which formerly adorned the Duomo (see CHURCHES 1, WALK 1, A-Z), the Battistero (see WALK 1, A-Z) and the Campanile (see WALK 1). There are works by Pisano (see A-Z), di Cambio and Donatello (see A-Z), as well as Michelangelo's (see A-Z) chilling *Pietà* which he executed at the age of 80 for his own tomb, and which was finished posthumously by Calcagni. See MUSEUMS 1.

**Museo di Storia della Scienza:** Originally called the Academy of Experimental Sciences and founded by Leopold de' Medici (1657) in the Palazzo Pitti (see A-Z), the museum reflects the depth of the Medici (see A-Z) and Lorraine families' interest in the sciences. The work of Galileo (see A-Z), who was much admired by the Medicis, occupies an important place here. See MUSEUMS 2.

**Museo Michelangelo:** The Casa Buonarroti was built by Michelangelo's nephew Leonardo Buonarroti, who inherited the site from his uncle. He in turn bequeathed the house to his son, Michelangelo the Younger, who built a gallery here in honour of his

famous great-uncle. It was finally made into a museum in 1858 by the last remaining member of the family, who passed it on to the city. It contains an interesting selection of early sculptures, facsimiles of architectural drawings and wax models by Michelangelo, as well as paintings and statues illustrating his life. Note the wooden model of the facade of S Lorenzo by Baccio d'Agnolo (1517). See **MUSEUMS 1**, **Michelangelo**.

**Museo Stibbert:** Eccentric traveller and artist Frederick Stibbert left his villa (at Via Stibbert 26, 3 km north of the city centre) and eclectic private collection to the British Government who in turn donated it to the city of Florence. The display of arms and armour is world-famous. The museum is open from 0900-1400 Mon.-Wed., Fri., Sat., and 0900-1300 Sun. and hol. There are guided tours on the hour. The entrance fee is L. 2000, but there is no charge on Sundays.

**Music:** The Teatro Comunale on the Corso Italia has a symphony season from Feb. to Apr. and Oct. to Nov.; an opera and ballet season in Dec. and Jan.; and hosts

the Maggio Musicale (Music Festival) in May and July. Tickets can be purchased from the box office at Corso Italia 16 (tel: 2779236) from 0900-1300 Tues.-Sun. and one hour before the performance begins. The Teatro della Pergola at Via della Pergola 12 (tel: 262690) is also the venue for some of the events in the Maggio Musicale calendar as well as chamber music concerts arranged by the Amici della Musica from Jan. to Apr. and Oct. to Dec.

The Estate Fiesolana (a festival of music, drama and films) is held annually from the end of June to the end of Aug. at several venues in Florence (eg Santa Croce and the courtyard of the Pitti) as well as in Fiesole (see **A-Z**).

For details of folk music performances contact the Centro Flog, Via C. Bibi 33 (tel: 472598). There are also several bars and clubs featuring jazz and piano music (see **NIGHTLIFE**). See **Events**, **What's on**.

**Newspapers:** Florence's daily newspapers are *La Nazione* and *La Gazzetta di Firenze;* both list events and programmes. Foreign newspapers are widely available from many kiosks around the centre and at the station. British ones are available on the afternoon of the day of publication. See **What's On**.

**Nightlife:** The main recreations in Florence on summer evenings are strolling along the streets window-shopping and admiring the sights, relaxing in one of the terraced cafés on the popular Piazza della Repubblica (see **CAFES**), eating out in one of the busy restaurants, or watching the street entertainers who come here from all over the world. Although there is not much in the way of formal nightlife in Florence, there are several nightclubs, piano bars, discos and sometimes open-air dances near the Viale Michelangelo. See **NIGHTLIFE**.

**Ognissanti:** Originally founded in the 13thC by a Benedictine order which manufactured wool, the church was rebuilt in the 17thC (the elegant campanile and the terracotta tympanum above the door are all that remain of the original edifice). The facade is a 19thC copy of Matteo Nigetti's Baroque facade. The interior houses some splendid frescoes by Ghirlandaio (see **A-Z**) - notably the *Madonna della Misericordia* who protects the Vespucci family (America was named after Amerigo Vespucci, an agent of the Medicis). Ghirlandaio's *Last Supper* can be seen next door in the convent refectory (see **ART 2**). See **CHURCHES 2**.

**Opening Times:** These vary enormously and change throughout the year, but generally:
Shops - 0830/0900-1200/1300 and 1530/1600-1900/1930 (food shops 1700-2000); closed Sun. and Sat. pm (summer), Mon. am (winter), food shops closed Wed. pm. See **SHOPPING**, **Best Buys**.
Churches - 0730/0800-1200/1300 and 1500/1530-1900. See **CHURCHES**, **Religious Services**.
Museums (State) - 0900-1400 (1300 Sun. and hol.) Tues.-Sun. Private museums also open in the afternoons including Mon. Note that ticket offices usually close half-an-hour to one hour before museums close. See **MUSEUMS**.
Banks - 0830-1330 Mon.-Fri. and sometimes 1445-1545 (some bureaux de change are also open Sat. am and the one in the station is open 0820-1900). See **Currency**, **Money**.
Post Offices (see **A-Z**) - 0815-1330 Mon.-Fri., 0815-1200 Sat. See **Public Holidays**.

**Orientation:** Equip yourself with a detailed street map with a good index on your arrival in the city (available from most newsagents and kiosks) for Florence is best explored on foot. You will notice that some street numbers are followed by an 'r' (stands for *rosso* or 'red') to distinguish between two premises at the same address.

**Orsanmichele:** Built on the site of an 8thC oratory, the present 14thC building was intended as a combined granary and oratory. Several architects including Talenti were involved in the rebuilding, supervised by one of the city's guilds. Other major guilds took on the decoration of the exterior and interior pillars. For the exterior ones they commissioned some outstanding sculptures. Notice for instance, on the

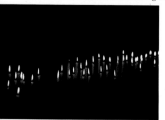

east facade, Ghiberti's (see **A-Z**) *Baptist* (1412-16) and Verrocchio's *Doubting Thomas* (c.1465-83). The south facade has a *St Mark* by Donatello (see **A-Z**), while Nanni di Banco was responsible for the *St Eligius* on the west facade and the *Quattro Coronati* on the north side. The interior columns are decorated by paintings of the patron saints of the guilds. The tabernacle by Orcagna (1355-9) was built to house Bernardo Daddi's miraculous *Virgin*. Go upstairs into what were the upper storage halls (the Saloni di Orsanmichele) for a wonderful view of the city. See **CHURCHES 2, WALK 1**.

**Palazzo Corsi:** This former residence of a wealthy family of cloth merchants, at Via de' Benci 6, has dye vats and drying areas. Today it houses the Horne Museum. See **MUSEUMS 1**.

**Palazzo Giugni:** This palace on the Via degli Alfani (No. 48) near SS Annunziata is one of Ammannati's finest buildings and has an exceptionally handsome wooden portal dating from the 16thC. Although the rest of the palace is closed to the public, the courtyard is usually accessible.

**Palazzo Medici-Riccardi:**
Commissioned by Cosimo de' Medici and built (1444–c.1460) by Michelozzo, the palace served as the Medicis' headquarters between 1464 and 1540, before they moved to the Palazzo Vecchio. The Riccardi family bought the palace in 1659 and enlarged it extensively. The architectural masterpiece of the building is the arcaded courtyard. The first staircase on the right leads to the chapel with its wonderful frescoes by Benozzo Gozzoli (see **ART 2**) and the second staircase leads to the gallery with its ceiling paintings of the *Apotheosis of the Medici Dynasty* by Luca Giordano (1682-3). The Medici Museum is off to the left. See **PALAZZI 1, WALK 2**.

**Palazzo Pitti:** The grandiose palace was built (1458-72) for the rich merchant Luca Pitti who was determined to display his wealth and power to the world. Eleonora di Toledo (wife of Cosimo I) bought the palace in 1550 and moved the grand-ducal residence here from the Palazzo Vecchio (see **PALAZZI 1, WALK 1, A-Z**), to which it is linked by Vasari's (see **A-Z**) Corridoio (tel: 218141 to book a visit to the Corridor). Ammannati was commissioned to extend the two wings. He also restructured the courtyard and had a hand in designing the gardens (see **Giardino di Boboli**). The palace and its gardens now contain some of Florence's most important museums and galleries (see **ART 1, MUSEUMS 3**). See **PALAZZI 1, WALK 1**.

**Palazzo della Signoria:** See Palazzo Vecchio.

**Palazzo Strozzi:** This huge rusticated palace took 47 years to build (1489-1536). The original design, probably by Giuliano da Sangallo, was greatly modified by Benedetto da Maiano and Cronaca, to whom the elegant courtyard loggia and cornice are attributed. The interior of

the building is less severe than the facade and houses various cultural
institutions as well as the Museo Piccolo which outlines the various
stages of the palace's construction (access through courtyard).
See **PALAZZI 1**.

**Palazzo Vecchio (Palazzo della Signoria):** This fortress-like
Town Hall's various changes of name reflect the changing forms of gov-
ernment experienced by the city since it was built in the 13th and
14thC. Originally called the Palazzo dei Priori after Florence's first
rulers (priors from the major guilds), it has also been known as the
Palazzo del Popolo, the Palazzo della Signoria and the Palazzo
Ducale, and has witnessed the changing fortunes of Savonarola (see
**A-Z**) and the Medicis (see **A-Z**). Its design is attributed to Arnolfo di
Cambio after whom the lofty bell-tower is named. Vasari (see **A-Z**) dec-

orated Michelozzo's courtyard and many of the lavish apartments in the 16thC. You can visit the Quartieri Monumentali (see **MUSEUMS 3**) and the remodelled Studiolo (study) di Francesco I. See **PALAZZI 1, WALK 1**.

**Parking:** Illegally parked cars are towed away, so be warned. To retrieve your car, go to the car pound at Via Circondaria 19 (tel: 351562). Use official car parks for security and convenience. These can be found at the Piazza della Stazione (central), the Porta Romana (on the left bank), the Cascine (Piazza Vittorio Veneto), the Fortezza da Basso, the Piazza del Carmine and Piazza del Cestello(left bank).

**Passports and Customs:** A valid passport (or identity card for some EC visitors) is necessary, but no visa is required for stays of less than three months. There is no limit on the amount of money you can bring in or out of the country, but amounts over a million lire must be declared on the V 2 form you fill out on entry. Any valuable antiques or objets d'art must be accompanied by an authorization of purchase from the Fine Arts Department (arranged by the shop where you bought it).

**Pazzi Conspiracy:** In 1478 members of the rival banking family, in league with Pope Sixtus IV, plotted to overthrow the Medicis (see **A-Z**) and take control of the city. The conspirators attacked Lorenzo and Giuliano in the Duomo (see **CHURCHES 1, WALK 1, A-Z**) as they were receiving the Sacrament, but only managed to kill the latter (the injured Lorenzo finding refuge in the sacristy). No mercy was shown to the conspirators once news of the foul deed was out - they were either executed on the spot or strung up in the Bargello (see **MUSEUMS 1, A-Z**) or the Palazzo Vecchio (see **PALAZZI 1, WALK 1, A-Z**).

**Pets:** Small pets which have been vaccinated for rabies (see **A-Z**) in the last year and have a health certificate are permitted into Italy.

**Piazza della SS Annunziata:** One of Florence's most harmonious square was further improved by Brunelleschi's (see **A-Z**) addition of the Loggia degli Innocenti, echoing the style of the earlier Loggia of the Confraternita dei Servi di Maria opposite (attributed to Baccio d'Agnolo, 1516-25). See **PIAZZE**, **Events**, **SS Annunziata**.

**Piazza Santa Croce:** The historic centre of the populous cloth dyers' quarter where the city's prosperity originated (and where 'houses of ill-fame' became established). Notice the Palazzo dell'Antella (1619) at No. 21 which is decorated with frescoes executed by 12 painters in 20 days under the supervision of Giovanni da S Giovanni. The Palazzo Serristori at No. 1 (opposite the church) is attributed to the architect Baccio d'Agnolo. See **CHURCHES 2**, **PIAZZE**, **WALK 1**, **Events**, **Santa Croce**.

**Piazza della Signoria:** Talenti's Loggia dei Lanzi flanks the fortress-like Palazzo Vecchio (see **PALAZZI 1**, **A-Z**) on the other side of the Piazzale degli Uffizi. Facing it, across the square, is the Romanesque facade of the Palazzo Uguccioni (see **PALAZZI 2**). To the left, on the north side of the *piazza*, is the 14thC Tribunale della Mercatanzia (Commercial Court). The *ringhiera*, from where politicians addressed the crowd, is still used today for political demonstrations. A block set in the paving stones in the centre marks the spot where Savonarola (see **A-Z**) was executed. See **PIAZZE**, **WALK 1**.

**Piazzale Michelangelo:** A beautiful terrace 100 m above the Arno which offers wonderful panoramas of the city, its surrounding country-side and even the distant Appenine peaks. It contains bronze reproductions of various works by Michelangelo *(see **A-Z**)* including his famous *David (see **A-Z**).*

**Pisa:** See **EXCURSION 2**.

**Pisano, Andrea (c.1290-1348/49):** The sculptor, goldsmith and architect who executed the first set of bronze doors for the Battistero (see **WALK 1**, **A-Z**) and supplied the upper portion of the Campanile (see **WALK 1**) with various statues and reliefs.

**Police:** There are various types of police in the city: the Vigili Urbani, who are responsible for traffic control and general administrative problems within the city (tel: 352141); the Carabinieri and Polizia, responsible for serious crimes and crowd control; and the Polizia Stradale (Road Police) who are concerned with traffic both inside and outside of town (tel: 577777). See **Emergency Numbers**.

**Ponte Vecchio:** The original 12thC edifice was swept away by the flood of 1333 and the present structure built to replace it in 1345. From the beginning it was intended as a shopping area. The tanners, butchers and other shopkeepers who set up businesses here were eventually expelled by Ferdinando I, who could not stand the smell of hides and carcasses as he traversed the elevated corridor above. Thereafter the bridge was restricted to goldsmiths' and jewellers' businesses, whose premises are still there today. See **WALKS 1 & 3**.

**Porta Romana:** One of the city's oldest gates, dating from 1326. It is decorated with a 14thC fresco of the Virgin. Located south of the Pitti Palace (see **ART 1**, **PALAZZI 1**, **WALK 1**, **Palazzo Pitti**) and the Giardino di Boboli (see **A-Z**), you can walk from here to Belvedere (see **CITY SIGHTS**) along the old city walls.

**Post Offices:** The Central Post Office, on the Via Pellicceria near the Piazza della Repubblica, has a 24-hr telegram and international phone service and poste restante facilities (0815-1900 Mon.-Fri., 0815-1300 Sat.). The other main post office for tourists is at Via Pietrapiana 53-55 (0815-1330 Mon.-Sat.). The telegram service is open 0815-1330 Mon.-Sat., and the international telephone service 0730-1930 Mon.-Fri., 0730-1330 Sat. The formalities for sending parcels abroad are complicated so ask at the post office for advice on the different types of parcel and the way each should be wrapped. Stamps are sold at tobacconists (displaying a 'T' sign) and hotels as well as post offices. The current rate for a postcard to any EC country is L. 550 (L. 550 plus L. 300 for every extra 5 g to the USA), while a letter under 20 g costs L. 650 (L. 750 plus L. 300 for every extra 5 g to the USA). Letter boxes are red. See **Opening Times**, **Telephones and Telegrams**.

**Public Holidays:** 1 Jan. (New Year); Easter Monday; 25 April (Liberation Day); 1 May (Labour Day); 24 June (St John's Day - see **Events**), 15 Aug. (Assumption); 1 Nov. (All Saints' Day); 8 Dec. (Immaculate Conception); 25 Dec. (Christmas Day); 26 Dec. (St Stephen's Day).

**Rabies:** Still exists here as in other parts of the Continent. As a pre-caution have all animal bites seen to by a doctor. See **Pets**.

**Railways:** S Maria Novella Station (Stazione Centrale) has direct links to all the main Italian cities including Rome, Milan, Naples and Genoa, as well as to Paris and Zurich and the German cities of Dortmund, Hamburg and Stuttgart. Services are reliable and reasonably priced (enquire about discounts). Tel: 278785 (0700-2200) or contact the EPT office for information (see **Tourist Information**). The fastest trains are the Trans Europe Express (TEE) and the Intercity (IC) which stop at major destinations only (reserve in advance). The Rapido (R) and Espresso (ES) are also express services and only stop at large towns. The Diretto (D), Locale (L), Accelerato (A) and Littorina (L) are all fairly slow local services which stop frequently. Tel: 212319 for the left-luggage office or 212296 for the railway police. Porters charge L. 700 per bag inside the station and L. 1650 from station to hotel. See **Tipping**.

**Raphael (1483-1520):** See ART 1, UFFIZI 2.

**Religious services:**
Roman Catholic Masses in English - the Duomo. 1700 Sat. (confessions are heard 0930-1045 Thurs., 1000-1200 Fri., and 15 min before Mass on Sat.); the church of Hospital of St John of God, Borgognissanti 16-20. 1000 Sun. & hol.
Church of England - St Mark's, Via Maggio 16 (tel: 294764). 0900 and 1030 Sun., 1000 Wed., 2000 Fri.
American Episcopal Church - St James's, Via B. Rucellai 9 (tel: 294417). 0800, 1100 Sun.
Jewish Synagogue - Via L. Farini 4 (tel: 245252). Sat. 0845, 1600 winter; 0830, 1700 summer.

Baptist Church - Evangelica Battista, Borgognissanti 6 (tel: 210537). 1100 Sun.

Lutheran Church - Chiesa Evangelica Luterana, Lungarno Torrigiani 11 (tel: 2342775). 1000 Sun.

Methodist Church - Chiesa Evangelica Metodista, Via dei Benci 9 (tel: 677462). 1100 Sun.

**Romanesque:** A style of European architecture which prevailed in the 11th and 12thC and is characterized by round arches, massive walls and groin vaults.

**San Felice:** The facade of this Gothic church, standing on the Piazza S Felice near the Palazzo Pitti (see PALAZZI 1, WALK 1, **A-Z**), is attributed to Michelozzo (1457). A large crucifix from Giotto's workshop hangs over the side door. You can visit the church daily 0800-1200, 1600-1830.

**San Gimignano:** See EXCURSION 3.

**San Lorenzo:** Financed by the Medici family, designed by Brunelleschi (see **A-Z**) and built between 1419 and 1469 on the site of two earlier churches, this imposing building was the first to be constructed in the Renaissance style. Michelangelo (see **A-Z**) was commissioned to complete the facade, but in fact it was never finished (you can see Baccio d'Angolo's model for it in the Museo Michelangelo - see MUSEUMS 1). The belfry is an 18thC addition. The harmonious interior houses several of the Medici family tombs. The Sagrestia Vecchia (Old Sacristy), to the left of the high altar, is one of Brunelleschi's (see **A-Z**) masterpieces and was richly decorated by Donatello (see **A-Z**). See CHURCHES 2, WALK 2, **Cappelle Medicee**.

**San Marco:** The present Dominican church and convent are built on the site of two earlier monasteries belonging to the Vallombrosan order. Cosimo the Elder took on the expense of the rebuilding in 1437 and commissioned Michelozzo as architect. Vasari (see **A-Z**) was responsible for the interior decoration of the church nave, Silvani for the wooden ceiling and Giambologna for the design of the chapel of S

Antonino. Apart from St Anthony, the monastery's most famous inhabitants were Savonarola (see **A-Z**) and Fra Angelico (see **A-Z**) - the building is now given over to a museum dedicated to the latter. There you can visit the dormitory containing 44 cells decorated with frescoes by Fra Angelico and his followers (look out in particular for his famous *Annunciation*). The chapter-room contains his *Crucifixion* and the Ospizio dei Pellegrini houses 20 of his panel paintings. There is also a remarkable 6thC mosaic of *The Virgin at Prayer*. See **CHURCHES 2, MUSEUMS 1, WALK 2**.

**San Miniato al Monte:** Located on a hill to the south east of the city, this is one of the oldest (11thC) and most attractive churches in Florence. Legend has it that Minias, a 3rdC martyr, is buried here, and the present church is said to stand on the site of a shrine which formerly protected his tomb. The fine interior, remarkable for its paving which resembles oriental embroidery, contains a superb chapel commemorating the Cardinal of Portugal, in which all the architectural and decorative elements are in complete harmony. See **CHURCHES 2, WALK 3**.

**Santa Croce:** From the outset, when Arnolfo di Cambio was commissioned to design this majestic building (c.1294), it was planned as one of the largest churches in the Christian world. Certainly it is the largest Franciscan church, having taken almost a century to complete (1294-1384). Its immense interior houses some 276 tombs of many of Florence's most celebrated figures, 19 chapels - including that of the Pazzi family (see **Cappella dei Pazzi**), the most beautiful cloisters in the city and the impressive Museo dell'Opera di S Croce (see **MUSEUMS 2**). Notable among its treasures are Rossellino's *Madonna* (1478), Benedetto da Maiano's marble pulpit (1474-75) and Donatello's (see **A-Z**) *Annunciation* (c.1435). The Peruzzi and Bardi Chapels contain frescoes by Giotto (see **A-Z**), and the Chancel has murals and stained glass by Agnolo Gaddi which depict the *Legend of the Finding of the True Cross* (the theme of which explains the church's name). See **CHURCHES 2, WALK 1**.

**Santa Felicità:** On the Piazza S Felicità, reached along the Via dei Guicciardini from the Palazzo Pitti (see **PALAZZI 1, WALK 1, A-Z**). Vasari (see **A-Z**) built a corridor over the church porch enabling Cosimo I to worship privately in the Palco Reale within. The Capella Capponi downstairs (by Brunelleschi - see **A-Z**) houses Pontormo's *Deposition* and *Annunciation*. Visits 0800-1200, 1600-1900. See **WALK 3**.

**Santa Maria del Carmine:** The building, by Ruggeri and Mannaioni, lacks real interest apart from a small museum in the cloister which houses frescoes by Starnina (fragments of others by him are in the Corsini Chapel) and Filippo Lippi (see **A-Z**). See **CHURCHES 1**.

**Santa Maria Maggiore:** Only the bell-tower on the left of the 13th-14thC Gothic facade of this church in the Via de' Cerretani, just west of the Battistero, remains from the earlier Romanesque structure. The interior Baroque facade is by Buontalenti, and there is a splendid 13thC altarpiece (in relief) of the *Madonna and Child* attributed to Coppo di Marcovaldo. The church is open daily 0700-1200, 1530-1930.

**Santa Maria Novella:** Dominican architects built the present church and convent (1246-1360) on the site of an older church which the order acquired some 20 years earlier. The Renaissance facade is by

Alberti. The most important work in the church is Masaccio's (see **A-Z**) influential fresco of *The Trinity* (c.1425). The Strozzi Chapel contains Nardo di Cione's frescoes of *The Last Judgement* (with a portrait of Dante), *Paradise* and the *Inferno*. The wooden crucifix within the marble Gondi Chapel is attributed to Brunelleschi (see **A-Z**). He also designed the marble pulpit. The Cappella Maggiore behind the altar has frescoes by Ghirlandaio (see **A-Z**). The Spanish Chapel was designed by Talenti for Eleanora of Toledo. See **CHURCHES 2, WALK 2**.

**Santa Trinità:** One of Florence's oldest churches, founded by the Vallombrosian order in the 11thC (notice the 17thC wooden doors carved with images of the order's saints). The present structure dates from the 13thC and has an unattractive 16thC facade by Buontalenti. The Gothic interior however is strikingly simple. The Sassetti Chapel (named after the manager of the Medici Bank whose tomb is contained within) houses some remarkable frescoes of *St Francis* and an altarpiece of *The Adoration of the Magi* by Ghirlandaio (see **A-Z**). The Scali Chapel on the other side of the chancel contains the marble tomb of Bishop Benozzo Federighi of Fiesole (1454-57), considered to be one of Luca della Robbia's finest works. See **CHURCHES 1**.

**Santissima Annunziata:**
The mother church of the Servite order, originally an oratory, was founded in 1234 by seven Florentine nobles on the site of an earlier Franciscan monastery, and was rebuilt by Michelozzo in the 15thC respecting the architectural harmony of the

*piazza* (see **PIAZZE***). It is one of Italy's most important shrines (the miraculous fresco of *The Annunciation* is housed in the *tempietta* to the left of the entrance). The central portal leads to the Chiostro dei Voti decorated with frescoes of *The Assumption* by Rosso (1517), *The Birth of the Virgin* (1513-14) and *The Voyage of the Magi* by Andrea del Sarto

(1511) and *The Nativity* by Baldovinetti (1460-2). The antrium is named after the life-sized wax effigies (*voti*) formerly left here by important visitors. The tribune was decorated by Giambologna for his own tomb and those of other Flemish painters who had resided in Florence. Andrea del Sarto is also buried here - look out for his delicate painting of *The Virgin with a Cushion* in the Chiostro dei Morti (entrance next to the church). See **CHURCHES 2**.

**Santo Spirito:** The present church (1434-87) was designed by Brunelleschi (see **A-Z**) who died before the building was completed. Construction continued under a series of architects who radically modified his plans for the exterior. The white facade was never finished, the red tiled cupola by Cronaca and Salvi d'Andrea was completed in 1482 and the bell-tower added between 1503 and 1517. The overall effect, however, is graceful. The magnificent interior conforms to the original plans and is one of the most delightful in Florence. Filippino Lippi's (see **A-Z**) splendid altarpiece of the Nerli family can be seen in the right transept, and a door under the organ leads to a remarkable vestibule by Cronaca (1492-94), through which you can gain access to Sangallo's octagonal sacristy (1488-96). See **CHURCHES 1**.

**Savonarola, Girolamo (1452-98):** The Dominican friar (prior of San Marco - see **CHURCHES 2, MUSEUMS 1, WALK 2, A-Z**) and evangelical reformer became leader of the democratic party after the Medicis (see **A-Z**) were expelled. His 'reign' lasted from 1494 to 1498 when he was excommunicated by Pope Alexander VI for his attacks on the corruption of the papacy and his support for Charles VIII of France. An eloquent, often brutal preacher, his main theme was the need to repent the decadence and vice of the age. Although uncompromising, he commanded the respect of many. He was finally imprisoned, hung and then burnt at the stake as a heretic.

**Shopping:** Most of the best (and most expensive) shops are to be found along the Via Tornabuoni as well as round the Piazza del Duomo (see **PIAZZE, WALK 1**) and the Piazza della Repubblica. Antique shops are concentrated around the Borgognissanti, Borgo San Iacopo, Via della

Vigna Nuova, Via della Spada and the Ponte Vecchio (see **WALKS 1 & 3**, **A-Z**), which also has small jewellery stores. There are numerous leather shops around Santa Croce (see **CHURCHES 2, WALK 1, PIAZZE, A-Z**) as well as a leather factory and more shops inside the church itself. It is worth trying to bargain for discounts, even in big shops, when you are buying several things at once. Most shops will be quite happy to arrange posting your purchases abroad. See **MARKETS, SHOPPING**, **Best Buys**, **Opening Times**.

**Siena:** The provincial capital of Tuscany. Pop: 65,600. Tourist Office: Piazza del Campo 55, tel: (0599) 280551.

The 'City of the Virgin' is named after the Roman colony Saena Julia which was founded here by Augustus on the site of an Etruscan settlement. Architecturally it is a Gothic city, having managed to avoid the influence of the Florentine Renaissance. It spreads out over three hills from the main Piazza del Campo (divided into nine sections representing the Guelph Council of Nine who ruled in the 13thC) and is surrounded by seven kilometres of walls with only eight of the original 38 gates surviving. The town's three main streets meet at the Croce del Travaglio. See **EXCURSION 1**.

**Smoking:** International brands are generally available, but cost about twice as much as Italian cigarettes - which are considerably stronger. Cigarettes, cigars and pipe tobacco are sold in bars and in shops with a 'T' sign. Try a *toscano*, a small black cigar popular with Florentines.

**Spedale degli Innocenti:** This complex, standing on the eastern side of the Piazza della SS Annunziata (see **PIAZZE**, **A-Z**), was designed by Brunelleschi (see **A-Z**) and commissioned by the Arte della Seta (Silk Guild). Work began on it in 1421. The arcade, which dominates the square, is a magnificent example of early Florentine Renaissance architecture. The name (O)spedale degli Innocenti originates from the building's intended function as a home for abandoned children. Inside, there are two very beautiful cloisters; indeed, the rectangular Chiostro delle Donne is one of the most interesting in Florence. The first floor houses an art gallery containing detached frescoes, illuminated 14th-15thC manuscripts and 18thC paintings (see **ART 1**).

**Sports:** Spectator sports:
Horse-racing - Hippodromo Visaro, Piazzale delle Cascine (tel: 360056); Hippodromo Le Mulina, Viale del Pegaso, tel: 411130).
Football (a favourite Italian sport) - Stadio Communale, Viale M. Fanti 4/6, tel: 587858).
Motor racing - International Formula 1 track at Autodromo del Mugello, Scaperia, tel: 846351).
Participatory sports:
Swimming - outdoor pools at Bellariva, Lungarno Colombo 6 (Bus 14); Costoli, Viale Paoli (Bus 17); Le Pavoniere, Viale degli Olmi, Parco delle Cascine (Bus 17).
Tennis - Viale Michelangelo 61, tel: 6811880 (book court in advance, no racket hire - Bus 13).
Golf - Golf dell'Ugolino, Via Chiantigiana 3, tel: 2301009 (you must be a member of another club to play here, hire of clubs: L. 30,000; fee: L. 50,000 during the week and L. 60,000 at weekends).

**Taxis:** There are taxi ranks outside Central Station (see **Railways**) and in all the main squares as well as at the Porta Romana (see **A-Z**). You can also phone for one (tel: 4390 or 4798 - costs extra), but you cannot hail one. Taxis are yellow or white in colour, are metered and are usually expensive. There is an extra charge at night and for each item of luggage. See **Transport**.

**Telephones and Telegrams:** You will find public telephones on many streets, at the station, in bars and newsagents (displaying the blue and yellow sign), at the Centro Telefonici Pubblico (SIP), Via Cavour 21, and in the main post offices (see **Post Offices**). Newer coin-operated phones take L. 100, 200 and 500 coins. Other phones operate on phone cards worth L. 1000 and 5000, which can be purchased at tobacconists, but some of the older ones still only accept tokens (*gettoni*) which can be purchased in bars, hotels, newsagents, tobacconists and post offices for L. 200.

It is best to make international calls from the main post offices or the SIP centre (0730-2130) where you pay for the number of units used at the end. To direct dial abroad, dial 00 followed by the code for the country (UK - 44, USA - 1), then remember to omit the first 0 of the city code.

| Directory Enquiries | tel: 12. |
| European Operator | tel: 15. |
| Intercontinental Operator | tel: 170. |

See also **Emergencies**.

There is a 24-hr telegram service at the head post office (see **Post Offices**), or you can send one by phone (tel: 186). A cheaper, more efficient alternative is a night letter/telegram which is guaranteed to arrive the following morning.

**Theatre:** See **Events**, **Music**.

**Time Difference:** 1 hr ahead of GMT.

**Tipping:** Although restaurant, café and hotel bills usually include a service charge, it is customary to leave a 10% tip. Taxi drivers, cinema and theatre ushers, hairdressers, toilet attendants and guides also expect to be tipped. Porters should be given L. 1000 per item of luggage.

**Titian (1480/85-1576):** See ART 1, UFFIZI 2.

**Toilets:** Public toilets are scarce, but you will find some in the Palazzo Vecchio (see PALAZZI 1, WALK 1, **A-Z**) and the Palazzo Pitti (PALAZZI 1, WALK 1, **A-Z**) as well as in some of the larger stores and restaurants and in the station. Be warned - standards of hygiene are not generally high.

**Tourist Information:** The Ente Nazionale per il Turismo (ENIT) offices will help you with any queries and advise you on such matters as accommodation. They also provide free maps. The regional office, Ente Provinciale per il Turismo (EPT), for Florence is at Via Manzoni 16, tel: 2478141 (0820-1340 Mon.-Fri., 0820-1330 Sat.). The regional office for Tuscany is at Via di Novoli 26, tel: 43821.
In addition, the Azienda Autonoma di Soggiorno e Turismo (AAST), Via Tornabuoni 15, tel: 217459 is responsible for coordinating the various regional agencies and functions as an information centre (0800-1400 Mon.-Sat., closed hol.). See **Accommodation**.

**Transport:** The most convenient way of getting around the city, apart

from walking (since nearly everything lies within a small radius), is by local bus. In summer you can usually hire (establish the fare before you set off) a horse-drawn carriage in the Piazza del Duomo (see **PIAZZE, WALK 1**) or the Piazza della Signoria (see **PIAZZE**, **WALK1**, **A-Z**), and daily coach tours of the city depart from the main hotels. To explore the Tuscan countryside you will either need to hire a car or book a coach excursion. There are also reliable bus and train services to destinations throughout the region. Intercity travel is best by train, which is extremely fast, reliable and good value. See **Airports**, **Buses**, **Driving**, **Guides**, **Railways**, **Taxis**.

**Traveller's Cheques:** See **Crime and Theft**, **Currency**, **Money**, **Opening Times**.

**Uccello, Paolo (1396/97-1475):** The techniques of perspective so intrigued this Florentine artist that he became almost obsessed with experimenting with double vanishing points, foreshortening and other devices for dramatic effect in his drawings and paintings. Look out for his large panel depicting *The Battle of San Romano* in the Uffizi (see **UFFIZI 1**, **WALK 1**, **A-Z**).

**Uffizi:** Vasari (see **A-Z**) began the construction of this elegant building in 1560 to house the administrative offices of Cosimo I. Today it contains restoration laboratories and one of the most famous museums in the world, the Galleria degli Uffizi (see **ART 1**, **UFFIZI**), filled with the prestigious Medici collections of Italian art (exhibited in chronological order). Look out for Room 18 in particular - this is the Sala della Tribuna, an octagonal windowless room designed by Buontalenti to display only the finest pieces in the collection. Visits to Vasari's Corridoio (doorway next to Room 34 on west corridor), containing a series of famous self-portraits, are by previous appointment only (see **Palazzo Pitti**). See **WALK 1**.

**Vasari, Giorgio (1511-74):** The Renaissance painter, architect and writer was born in Arezzo (see **EXCURSION 1**, **A-Z**). He received his artistic training in the workshop of Andrea del Sarto in Florence before moving to Rome and embarking on decorations to the Vatican. On his return to Florence he designed the Uffizi (see **UFFIZI**, **WALK1**, **A-Z**) and painted the frescoes in the Palazzo Vecchio's Sala Grande (see **PALAZZI 1**, **A-Z**). He is chiefly remembered for his seminal book of art criticism *Lives of the Most Eminent Painters, Sculptors and Artists* (pub. 1550). See **CHURCHES 1**.

**Volterra:** See **EXCURSION 3**.

**What's on:** The Azienda Autonoma (see **Tourist Information**) distribute a free listings magazine published every two months called *Firenze Oggi* (Florence Today) which contains theatre and cinema programmes and information on festivals and other events. It is printed in English and Italian. There are also two weekly magazines, *Firenze Sera* and *Firenze Spettacolo* which give a complete programme of all the events, exhibitions, concerts and public performances. See **Events, Newspapers**.

**Youth Hostels:** You will need a membership card to stay in one of Florence's four Ostelli della Gioventù. If you do not already have one you can obtain one from the Italian Association of Youth Hostels, Viale

Augusto Righi 2 (tel: 610300). The adjacent hostel at the Villa Camerata has 29 rooms and is open all year (tel: 601451). It costs L. 9000 per night, inclusive of breakfast.

GALLERIA
DEGLI
UFFIZI